ARTHUR FOOTE

1853–1937

An Autobiography

Da Capo Press Music Reprint Series

MUSIC EDITOR

BEA FRIEDLAND

Ph.D., City University of New York

ARTHUR FOOTE

1853–1937

An Autobiography

With a New Introduction and Notes by
Wilma Reid Cipolla

DA CAPO PRESS • NEW YORK • 1979

Library of Congress Cataloging in Publication Data

Foote, Arthur William, 1853-1937.
  Arthur Foote, 1853-1937.

  (Da Capo Press music reprint series)
  Reprint of the 1946 ed. priv. print. at Plimpton
Press, 1946.
  Includes indexes.
  1. Foote, Arthur William, 1853-1937. 2. Composers
— United States — Biography.
ML410.F75A3   1979   780'.92'4 [B]   78-2021
ISBN 0-306-77531-X

This Da Capo Press edition of *Arthur Foote (1853-1937): An Autobiography*
is an unabridged republication, apart from new material prepared especially
for this edition by Wilma Reid Cipolla, of the first edition
published in Norwood, Mass., in 1946.

Published by Da Capo Press Inc.
A Subsidiary of Plenum Publishing Corporation
227 West 17th Street, New York, N.Y. 10011

INTRODUCTION

The primary printed source of information on the American composer Arthur William Foote (1853-1937) is his *Autobiography,* written in 1927 and privately distributed by his daughter, Katharine Foote Raffy, to a small group of friends and institutions in 1946. Aside from two unpublished dissertations,[1] Foote has received limited attention from historians despite his prominent position in American music.[2] His fame rests, to a great extent, upon a few commonly accepted "firsts": 1) he was the first American composer to receive his entire musical training in the United States; 2) he obtained the first Master's degree in music to be granted by an American university; and 3) he was the first native-born and -trained American composer to achieve international recognition, as a member of the so-called "Boston Group." These statements, factual as they may be, require closer examination, for in themselves they do not serve as sufficient reasons for placing Foote in the pantheon of American musicians.

[1] Frederick Kopp, *Arthur Foote: American Theorist and Composer* (Ph.D. dissertation: University of Rochester, 1957); Doric Alviani, *The Choral Church Music of Arthur William Foote* (S.M.D. dissertation: Union Theological Seminary, 1962).

[2] *A Catalog of the Works of Arthur William Foote,* by Wilma Reid Cipolla is to be published as no. 5 in the College Music Society series, *Bibliographies in American Music* (Detroit, Mich.: Information Coordinators).

INTRODUCTION

Although Arthur Foote did not undertake the formal period of European study which was almost mandatory for the times, the training he did receive was altogether European in its orientation. Throughout the *Autobiography* Foote reiterated his indebtedness to men like Otto Dresel (1826-1890), Franz Kneisel (1865-1926), George Henschel (1850-1934), and Wilhelm Gericke (1845-1925);[3] and he gave credit to John Sullivan Dwight's European-focused *Journal of Music* for "its influence on my taste and knowledge."[4] The German-born or -trained musicians active in Boston during the early part of Foote's professional life certainly had as profound an influence on his music as the lessons in harmony and composition he received from Stephen Emery (1841-1891) and John Knowles Paine (1839-1906), who were also products of the Germanic tradition. His musicianship was further developed through piano and organ study with Benjamin Lang (1837-1909), the influential Boston conductor and friend of Wagner, with whom Foote traveled to Europe to attend the first Bayreuth Festival. In all, he made eight trips abroad over a twenty-year period between 1876 and 1897, coming into contact with many of the leading artists of the day.

On the second point, it is a fact that Arthur Foote was awarded the first Master's degree in music in the United States, but no official records of his graduate work — nor

[3] Arthur Foote, *Autobiography,* see esp. 113.
[4] *Ibid.,* 23.

vi

indeed of Harvard's course offerings for a graduate degree in music in 1874-1875 — have turned up to date. Although John Knowles Paine had been appointed in 1862 to teach music courses at Harvard, the professorship in music was not created until after Foote finished, when a graduate curriculum was first officially listed in the catalog. According to Kopp's investigations, it is entirely possible that Foote took only one undergraduate and one graduate course in counterpoint and fugue, both with Paine.[5] Foote's M.A. appears to have been granted on the basis of a paper on vocal music[6] and a final examination in counterpoint, fugue, and history, rather than on a planned sequence of course work. From a perusal of the thesis and examination questions, Kopp adjudges the level of work preliminary, suggesting that Foote was essentially a self-taught musician:

> He had a tremendous capacity for learning through observation and association with other musicians . . . His willingness to accept advice and criticism, his lifetime habit of self-analysis, and his constant interest in and study of music by other composers were important elements of his training as a composer.[7]

Various authorities on American music have used the term "Boston Group" as a convenient means of classifying Arthur Foote, George Chadwick (1854-1931),

[5] Kopp, *Arthur Foote*, 46, 52-55, 55n.
[6] Arthur W. Foote, *The Development of the Secular Style in Music* (M.A. thesis: Harvard College, 1875).
[7] Kopp, *Arthur Foote*, 55.

INTRODUCTION

Horatio Parker (1863-1919), Arthur Whiting (1861-1936), Mrs. H. H. A. Beach (1867-1944), and others,[2] but there is little justification for assuming that their associations were formal enough to constitute a regional school of composition. The designation is valid only on the basis of "common inheritance, attitudes, and general style"[9] or "homogeneous cultural and aesthetic background."[10] Foote was quite casual about the significance of his infrequent meetings, extending over a period of no more than four or five years,[11] at the St. Botolph Club with Chadwick, Parker, and Whiting, and he expressed himself clearly on the lack of any conscious effort within the group to develop a common native style:

> Boston...was...beginning to assert itself as a musically-creative centre, especially in the years 1880-1895. In 1890, to be specific, we had living with us Mrs. Beach, Bullard, Chadwick, Miss Lang, Griffes, MacDowell, Nevin, Paine, Horatio Parker, J. C. D. Parker, Mrs. Rogers, George E. Whiting, Arthur Whiting, Arthur Weld, and others ... although we cannot claim that a genuine, characteristic school of American music has yet developed, nor that there are any marked signs of such an event, we can yet feel

[8] Cf. H. Wiley Hitchcock's use of the term "Second New England School," in *Music in the United States: A Historical Introduction* (2d ed.; Englewood Cliffs, NJ: Prentice-Hall, 1974), 132.

[9] *Ibid.*

[10] Gilbert Chase, *America's Music* (rev. 2d ed.; NY: McGraw-Hill, 1966), 366.

[11] See Foote, *Autobiography*, 55, and his "A Bostonian Remembers," *The Musical Quarterly* 23/1 (Jan 1937), 41.

that there is a fairly large group of composers producing music that is extremely worthwhile.[12]

The salient point here is not so much Foote's inclusion
in the Boston group (nor the putatively "American" fla-
vor of his music) as the international recognition accorded
him as an esteemed American composer. The *Autobiography* presents the picture of a man whose stature abroad
was such that he was admitted to the inner circle of
musicians in England, as well as on the Continent. This
recognition, based on genuine admiration for his music,
to be sure, was reinforced by the wide distribution his
publications received. His American publisher, Arthur
P. Schmidt, had agreements with a number of European
houses which insured a ready market for Foote compositions[13] and fostered performance opportunities in London, Paris, Leipzig, Vienna, and Berlin.

Foote's position as an international figure is undis-
puted, yet the *Autobiography* reveals an unusual humil-
ity regarding his achievements as a composer. Foote referred to his early efforts as "reminiscent and rather of a
stencil pattern," "commonplace," "old-fashioned," and

---

[12] Foote, "Thirty-five Years of Music in Boston," *Harvard Musical Review* 1/1 (Oct 1912), 9-10.

[13] Schmidt issued many Foote publications in Europe under the follow-
ing imprints: Augener & Co. (London), Boosey & Co. (London), Breitkopf
und Härtel (Leipzig, London), August Cranz (Hamburg), J. Curwen & Sons
(London), F. Durdilly (Paris), A. Lengnick & Co. (London), Henry Litolff's
Verlag (Braunschweig), B. Schott's Söhne (Mainz, London), and J. Williams
(London).

acknowledged that he "knew little about orchestration."[14] He was keenly aware of the limits of his abilities and exceedingly modest about the ultimate value of his work.

Gilbert Chase's description of Foote and his colleagues as academics, classicists, and followers of Brahms[15] is supported by Foote's own self-assessment:

> ... my influences from the beginning, as well as my predilection, were ultra-conservative ... My harmony was correct but with little variety, the structure of my pieces conventional ... although deeply moved by Wagner, I did not have sense enough for a long time to learn from his music, and was late in appreciating the early Debussy.[16]

Such comments tend to obscure the authentic skill and craftsmanship distinguishing Foote's best works. Close examination of his music discloses a variety of tendencies, all of which place him firmly in the romantic tradition.[17] His chamber music, true, is akin to Brahms, but his piano music also reflects a familiarity with Schumann. Orchestral works such as the *Suite,* Op. 63 reveal a strong Tchaikovsky influence, and one can detect signs of Dvorak in the *Suite,* Op. 36. The *Four Character Pieces after Omar Khayyám,* Op. 48, which Foote considered his most successful work for orchestra, dis-

[14] Foote, *Autobiography,* 55-56.
[15] Chase, *America's Music,* 365-67.
[16] Foote, *Autobiography,* 57-58.
[17] See also Hitchcock, *Music in the United States,* 139.

plays a Lisztian rhythmic drive and a flair for instrumental color in the manner of Rimsky-Korsakov. Foote's strong melodic gift, as exemplified in the song, *I'm wearing awa'*, recalls the English folk-song tradition.

These descriptive comparisons are not meant to suggest that Foote's music is derivative and lacking in individuality, but rather to concur with Moses Smith's statement that "like most sentient beings, including even genius, he was a man of his time."[18] And to place "his time" in perspective, it must be noted that he began his career when Mendelssohn, Schumann, and Chopin were "pretty nearly in the class of novelties," that he heard the Schubert *Unfinished Symphony* "within a year after the discovery of its MS. in Vienna,"[19] and attended "the first (MS.) performance by Von Bülow of the Tschaikowsky Concerto."[20]

In addition to the three "firsts" by which he is commonly known, an evaluation of Foote's unique contribution to the development of American music must take into account his activities in three important areas — concert life, music education, and professional organizations. His efforts to promote concert life in Boston began early in his career, but here again, his modesty forces us to read between the lines of the *Autobiography* to gauge accurately his role in bringing music to the

[18] Foote, *Autobiography*, 126.
[19] *Ibid.*, 107.
[20] *Ibid.*, 44.

people of Boston. For several years he was a member of the program committee of the Harvard Musical Association, an organization whose concert series in the period 1865-1881 prefigured the Boston Symphony Orchestra. Foote later reminisced:

> ... it is good to look at the symphony concerts given for seventeen years, up to the beginning of the Boston Symphony Concerts, for they were the work of the Harvard Musical Association, and it was largely through them that a public was educated for the later ones.[21]

And further:

> Our orchestral concerts gave to most of us the only opportunity of acquaintance with the music of the great composers, with the exception of the concerts of the Handel and Haydn Society and of sporadic visits of artists, few indeed in those days.[22]

Besides this life-long involvement with the Harvard Musical Association, Foote himself organized and performed in numerous chamber music concerts between 1880 and 1895. Although his concerts emphasized the new music from Europe, they also included his own works and those of his American contemporaries.

In all likelihood, Foote's most influential role in American musical life has been in the field of music education. It is clear from a study of his career that he felt an obligation to support the best in music through teaching, as

[21] Foote, "Thirty-five Years of Music in Boston," *Harvard Musical Review* 1/1 (Oct 1912), 10.

[22] Foote, [Reminiscences], *Bulletin of the Harvard Musical Association* no. 4 (Dec 1935), [2].

well as in his concert activities. His livelihood was derived mainly from private piano instruction, first in his pupils' homes and then on a schedule which kept him in his studio almost nine hours daily. Those who benefited from personal study with him, either in private lessons or later in his classes at the New England Conservatory, were imbued with his devotion to high standards. Many of them were teachers themselves, thereby perpetuating his values by transmitting them to their students in turn.

One outgrowth of his pedagogical philosophy was a conscientious effort to provide good repertoire on all levels. This led him to edit or arrange an enormous number of piano pieces, published by Schmidt under Foote's own name as well as under the pseudonyms "Ferdinand Meyer" and "Carl Erich." Most of these works were by the fashionable composers of the day — Joseph Joachim Raff, Anton Rubinstein, Moritz Moszkowski, Benjamin Godard, Cécile Chaminade — but the most significant aspect of the contribution remains his editions of Bach, Handel, Beethoven, and Mozart, which appeared at a time when the great classics were not the standard student fare.

Foote's pedagogical interests were not confined to piano instruction, but extended to theoretical writings. His major work, the *Foote and Spalding Harmony*,[23] has

[23] Foote and Walter R. Spalding, *Foote and Spalding Harmony: Formerly Published as Modern Harmony in its Theory and Practice* (Evanston, Ill.: A. P. Schmidt Co., 1969).

been so successful that his reputation as a theorist perhaps overshadows his stature as a composer. It is curious that he slighted this phase of his work in the *Autobiography,* with no mention of the harmony text and only one brief reference[24] to his other theory treatise, *Modulation and Related Harmonic Questions.*[25] Its discussion of third-relationship, an important aspect of his own harmonic vocabulary, is noteworthy as the first treatment of this topic in an English language text.[26] Numerous didactic articles on a variety of subjects also appeared in the *Etude,* a primary medium for self-instruction in the early twentieth century. His nationwide distinction as a educator was such that he was offered a permanent appointment as chairman of the music department of the University of California at Berkeley, following his success as visiting professor there in 1911. His modesty and independent character prompted him to refuse that position, and kept him from accepting a post at the New England Conservatory until quite late in his career.

Foote's concern for the quality of American musical life was further represented by his support of numerous professional organizations, in particular his participation in the American Guild of Organists and the Music Teachers' National Association during their formative years.

---

[24] Foote, *Autobiography,* 106.
[25] Foote, *Modulation and Related Harmonic Questions* (Boston, NY: The Arthur P. Schmidt Co., 1919).
[26] Kopp, *Arthur Foote,* 119, 229-30n.

He was one of the founders of the A.G.O. in 1896 and served as its national president from 1909 to 1912. He became a member of the M.T.N.A. in 1884, eight years after its founding in 1876, and was active on several important committees, including the Examining Committee on American Compositions, for over twenty years. The 1884 meeting is significant in the history of American music, for it marked "the beginning of the first organized movement to encourage the American composer,"[27] with the program of all American compositions by Calixa Lavalée on 3 July. This concert, which Sumner Salter cites as the third such program given in the United States,[28] followed by seven years Annette Essipoff-Leschetizky's "American" concert in Boston in 1877, and like the earlier one, also included Foote's *Gavotte* for piano, Op. 3. The important of the M.T.N.A. as a champion of the American composer, especially between 1884 and 1890, is strongly stated by Sumner Salter:

> A fairly careful survey of the development of musical composition in America unquestionably leads to the conclusion that the M.T.N.A. is entitled to the credit of the first organized effort and the most effective early influence in promoting the interest of American musical composition . . .[29]

[27] Sumner Salter, "The Music Teachers' National Association in its Early Relation to American Composers," *MTNA Volume of Proceedings* 27 (1932), 14.
[28] *Ibid.*, 15.
[29] *Ibid.*, 9.

and echoed by Arthur Foote:

> As to the help the M.T.N.A. gave to us, it was invaluable *at the time,* in those important concerts — the '80's and '90's — (e.g. Indianapolis, Detroit) . . . The M.T.N.A. gave a chance to composers to show what they could do, and made their names known far and wide.[30]

The *Autobiography* is a valuable source of information about American music during an important time in our cultural history. Foote indicates some of the difficulties faced by native composers when he pays tribute to the leading conductors of the period for their willingness to program American compositions,[31] to Arthur P. Schmidt for his farsightedness in publishing American works,[32] and to the Music Teachers' National Association for its encouragement.[33] His comments on the introduction of new music to Boston audiences and the efforts to develop higher standards of performance reveal much about American taste and level of cultural sophistication in that era. As the personal reminiscence of a leading American composer, it presents a first-hand description of the status of serious music in Boston in the late nineteenth century.

The lack of a published biography of Arthur Foote makes the present reissue imperative, although this

[30] *Ibid.,* 16.
[31] Foote, [Reminiscences], *Bulletin of the Harvard Musical Association* no. 4 (Dec 1935), [2].
[32] Foote, *Autobiography,* 50-51, and "A Bostonian Remembers," *The Musical Quarterly* 23/1 (Jan 1937), 41.
[33] Foote, *Autobiography,* 50-51.

autobiography was not originally intended for publication. Explanatory notes have been added after the *Autobiography* in this reprint edition, referring back to pages in the text for which clarification, correction, or additional information seemed appropriate. There is also a Chronology which draws together the important events in Foote's life and career described in various contexts throughout the narrative. The Index of Names is an important addendum, since the *Autobiography* abounds in personal glimpses into the lives of a great many musicians well-known in Foote's day, but virtually forgotten now. The Index of Compositions is not a comprehensive list of works, since it includes only those titles to which Foote made reference in the text; the editor's catalog should be consulted for a complete bibliography (see footnote 2).

WILMA REID CIPOLLA
November 1, 1977

Arthur Foote

1853–1937

BUST BY COURTENAY POLLOCK, 1912

ARTHUR FOOTE

1853–1937

An Autobiography

Privately Printed at the
Plimpton Press · Norwood · Massachusetts
1946

CONTENTS

FOREWORD

My FATHER WROTE THIS AUTOBIOGRAPHY AT OUR farm in South Hampton, New Hampshire. It does not extend much beyond 1926, and was written primarily for me, with no thought of publication. After his death, however, my mother felt that it would interest not only his pupils and friends but also the many who knew him through his music alone. The war and the inception of my mother's long and fatal illness prevented the making of a larger book, begun with the help of Moses Smith, but the autobiography was complete, and now goes, as my mother ardently desired, to all who knew and loved my father.

KATHARINE FOOTE RAFFY

Kezar Falls, Maine
October 9, 1945

Autobiography

I·BEGINNINGS AND BOYHOOD

THERE HAD BEEN FIVE OTHER CHILDREN, AND FOR three the little grave-stones in Harmony Grove Cemetery mark the short lives. Henry Wilder and Mary White were living when I was born March 5, 1853, in a small and (for the period) comfortable house at 44 Warren Street, Salem. Because of my mother's death in 1857, and of my brother's becoming in 1861 the minister of King's Chapel, Boston, there were, as I grew up, only my father and sister Mary, who, though in 1857 a girl of fourteen, was my " little mamma." In 1866 my sister married John B. Tileston, and for some years they lived with us.

The house (destroyed in the Salem fire, July, 1914) was on the edge of the Chestnut Street district, lying at the entrance of the turnpike from Salem to Lynn and Boston, through which the trolley now runs. On this road there were at that time simply a few scattered farms between Salem and Lynn, and, about a mile from us, a toll-gate, even then one of the few left. Just before reaching Lynn there was the famous floating bridge of wood, resting on the water without supports underneath — water, to our boyish minds, of unfathomable depth (this was the bridge that Jumbo, Barnum's famous elephant, refused to cross, deeming it untrustworthy). To the west, covering the sides of Gallow's Hill (where the witches were hanged, according to tradition), and to the north, for a large part of Boston Street, were tanneries of a characteristic odor, to me rather pleasant. The North and South rivers bounding Salem were even then beginning to fill up (in the case of the South river to be filled intentionally for building purposes), but they were still reasonably clean; so that at that time we did not have the unpleasant smell from the North river that later became a nuisance.

In my father's large garden were apple, pear, and peach trees; currant, blackberry, and gooseberry bushes; with beautiful borders of box. Of the pear trees, three were given to me by my father as my own. Forty years or so before, a skilled Belgian gardener had been imported (I understood by the Francis Peabodys of that generation). This gardener not only showed people how to do things, but introduced a number of pears and other fruits, so that the gardens of Salem were unusual in their excellence and variety. It was, by the way, a common thing for grapevines — chiefly of the Isabella variety, which needs more heat than others — to be trained to climb over southern walls of the houses.

Salem in those days was a delightful place to live in. There was contentment and good average prosperity; with small incomes there was still ease. The richer people, though in beautiful houses and with much comfort, were singularly without ostentation. All wages were indeed small in comparison with those of today. Labor troubles were unknown. There was greater happiness, I think, in the lives of those who work with their hands. Thoughtful persons have for years realized that the great disproportion in what is got out of life by the poorer and richer groups was bound to disappear by degrees — something such of us as have lived until the present century have seen come to pass. But in the early years of my life the old conditions still existed. It was then, for instance, an easy thing for the people living in the fine great houses of Salem, Newburyport, and Portsmouth to run them comfortably, with plenty of service. Today, as we know, the situation is different, such houses being now nearly unsalable for this reason. There were the George Peabody house on Washington Square (now the Salem Club) ; the Pickman place on Chestnut Street (which was not only an enormous house with a big barn, large garden and greenhouses, but which also had, on the street behind, another walled-in garden of several acres, full of fruit trees) ; and the Cabot house next door, which was said to have sixty closets. Opposite the Cabot house, on the other side of Chestnut Street, was an enormous bed of tulips in the Cabot garden, for the flowering of which we watched every year. Then there was the Francis Peabody house on Essex Street, the site of the present Armory. Of this house my clearest recollection is its rather large garden.

Salem was then a city of about 20,000, a very good class of Irish being the only addition to the old inhabitants of English descent. It was well governed and its affairs well managed, the mayors being such men as Robert Rantoul, S. Endicott Peabody, John Robinson, and Arthur Huntington. We had one series of first-rate lectures and another consisting partly of lectures and partly of good concerts. We had a life of our own, and were not dependent upon Boston.

There were a few summer places at Beverly (Pickman, Burgess, Silsbee, Cabot, etc.) ; but nearly everybody stayed in town through the hot weather, and possibly took a short holiday. We youngsters had few of the amusements so common today. Golf was unknown here until much later. Tennis did not begin with us until after I graduated from college, my classmate, Jim Dwight, being identified with its development. Football (as the game is now) did not exist, although we did have a game in which a ball was kicked about. And in my college years there was a football " ten," but it was a very simple and boyish affair. Baseball was common, to be sure, but a very different game from that of today. There were sailing and rowing; and I used to like to row a dory down Beverly harbor or up to Danversport. At one time, for a few years, we had a riding school in the town, but it did not last. There was a gymnasium, too, where I grew rather expert at the trapeze, although I was poor in feats of strength, having then, as now, small muscular ability. I used to enjoy a dancing class for some years at Hamilton Hall on Chestnut Street (built in the 1820's and named after Alexander Hamilton). The famous Papanti was the teacher. My playmates, especially until I left the private school mentioned later, were naturally the boys of the neighborhood: Jack and Frank Peabody, George Silsbee, " Chud " Tuckerman, and Dudley Pickman. The Silsbee and Tuckerman families of that generation are all gone (of the Tuckermans, three brothers and a sister). In later life, while our paths diverged, the old feeling never lapsed.

For a town of our size four Unitarian churches seem a good many, and so it must have been found, because later they became two. That was the hey-day of the old Unitarianism. St. Peter's downtown was the only Episcopal church until Grace Church on Essex

Street was built, in my boyhood. We were Unitarians and went to the North Church. In the spring of 1929 I sat again in my father's pew, and heard my dear brother's boy, the Rev. H. W. Foote, make the address at the Church's centenary. At the same time Mr. George J. Perry played two of my anthems. Edmund B. Willson was the minister of the North Church during my youth and until 1895. He was a dear man, later venerable in appearance, with white side-whiskers; and his son Bob [1] was a pal of mine. One of my dim recollections is of my nurse Bridget taking me to the Catholic Church on Federal Street. So it is clear that even then there were many Catholics in Salem. The North Church, by the way, was built from the plans of an English church which were brought back from England about 1824 by Francis Peabody.

Our communication with Boston was by the Eastern Railroad (later absorbed by the rival Boston and Maine), and the running time to Boston was forty-five minutes. The engines all had names then, not numbers, and were handsome affairs though small, trains naturally being fewer in number than now. I had a boyish craze about locomotives, and knew all the names by heart, my ambition being, in fact, to become an engineer. Horse-cars were just beginning,

[1] Robert W. Willson, later Professor of Astronomy at Harvard College.

and one of the first lines ran between Salem and Peabody (South Danvers then). It's a small thing, but
shows a side of life that is curious, that on Sundays,
after church, all the men gathered at the post-office
and talked together until about 12.30, when a chaise
arrived with letters and copies of the *Saturday Evening Gazette* (the only Sunday paper, which had come
to Lynn from Boston by horse-car and thence to us).
And on Saturday afternoons I would open the garden
gate, and, crossing the street, leave a pot of beans to
be baked and called for the next morning — one of
several hundred pots (for baked beans were an in-
evitable Sunday breakfast).

Behind our garden, on Essex Street, was a hydrant
at which on Saturday afternoons the fire-engine
(worked by hand) often had a practice. Sometimes I
was one of a number of men and boys who pulled
hard on the bar which served as a lever to pump the
water. The pipes of the aqueduct were then wooden,
by the way. Ice for domestic purposes was from the
famous Wenham Lake, but was not in universal use
at that time. There is a curious story in this connection: the Tudor of that period had the idea of export-
ing ice to foreign countries (a mad thing it seemed
to people), and really laid the foundation of the
family fortune by the first and successful venture of
this sort. In the early morning, cows could be seen

[17]

coming in small and large groups up Essex or Warren Street, passing our house and going into the
Great Pasture, as the unoccupied land between Salem
and Lynn was called. In the evening the same cows in
procession began to move towards their several desti-
nations, this time starting all together — an odd
thing to look back to. It was said that the crooked
Essex Street, like some Boston streets, was traced in
the beginning by a cow.

As to my schooling, first it was at Ma'am Baker's
children's school next door to the John C. Lee house
on Chestnut Street, and after that at " Daddy
Waters' " boys' school by Salem Common. Waters
was the brother of Henry Fitz Waters, afterwards so
well known through his genealogical investigations
in England (where I saw him in 1879), especially as
regards John Harvard. The school was an easy-going
place, where apparently we learned little, since my
father took me away when I was between eleven and
twelve and placed me in the Hacker Grammar School,
where my brother had been before me. This
change was no doubt good as to education, but had
an unfortunate side in that it took me away
from daily association with the boys who had
been my playmates, and I lost contact with them
for a while.

At the Hacker School I had to enter much lower

than should have been the case, owing to the poor previous training. But I quickly ran through the other grades to the first class (I think in less than a year) , thence going to the High School, in which, for the last two years of the course, we had a fine teacher and man, John W. Perkins (afterwards principal of Dummer Academy, Byfield) as the Headmaster. As at college later, I had pretty good marks, doubtless absorbing a certain amount of knowledge. But in both cases I was never taught to think or observe, these qualities, to whatever degree I possess them, coming later in life. The truth is that we merely learned to recite, retaining little when classes were over. I believe that the only place where at that time one really was educated was the (new) Massachusetts Institute of Technology, which then, as now, set a high standard.

In the High School (where my familiars were Ernest and Billy Fenollosa, Fred Emerton, Frank Spinney, George Jewett, and Lewis Osborne) I played the piano when the classes marched in to take their places at their desks. Some of the boys mentioned above formed a little society, the ΠΦ, the main purpose of which was a quasi-newspaper, of which we were editors in turn, and for which we all wrote poems, essays and so forth. My part was the musical and theatrical criticism. There was a little shop op-

posite the school where I used to buy three-cent turn-
overs, mince and apple, and Salem " Gibraltars " and
" Black-Jacks." The former were a famous local pro-
duct of very hard and delicious candy; the Black-
Jacks were the kind you suck.

II · MUSIC

WHEN ABOUT TWELVE I BEGAN TO SHOW SIGNS OF interest in music, probably stimulated by my sister's lessons with Manuel Fenollosa, *the* teacher of Salem and its neighborhood. I had no especial musical inheritance or surroundings. My teacher was Miss Fanny Paine, a pupil of Lang; the instruction book was "Richardson's New Method" (which I now know was a really good one); and I made rapid progress. Our piano was a "square" Chickering, with very light but good action; and my favorite show-piece was a sort of finger tremolo (rapidly repeated notes), which today I should find nearly impossible with our heavier and deeper action. But "progress" meant merely playing notes faster; no idea of phrasing, pedalling, or expression. About two years later, Miss Paine took me to Boston to play to Lang, probably with some pride. After performing the Chopin A-flat Ballade to her and my satisfaction, I remember asking Lang what those curved lines (slurs) above the notes meant. Lang sent me to Stephen A. Emery at the New England Conservatory for harmony lessons. Very likely I showed him some of my attempts at composition — "The Sands of Dee" and so forth.

At the Conservatory there were three in my class (one of them a colored girl), but by the time we got half-way through the book (Richter) I was left alone.

In Salem at that time (about 1869) there were two men who were interested in such musical promise as was then apparent in me: Henry K. Oliver (composer of the well-known tune, " Federal Street "), whose musical output consisted of hymn-tunes. which he published in oblong volumes; and Dr. Francis Tuckerman, father of my friend " Chud," a gifted amateur, in that what he did was a by-product. His ability to write was instinctive rather than scholastic, and his desire to compose was a good deal the result of his having charge of the music at Grace Church, where he sang tenor. They were both extremely kind to me, and I now see that their encouragement had great influence on my future. To show our point of view at that time, it is perhaps most significant that our favorite pieces were the Mendelssohn " Songs without Words," of which Lang had played for the first time the posthumous work (No. 7) in a concert at Salem a little while before.

Schumann is dated for me by my discovering, in the supplement of a New York musical journal, one of the " Kreisleriana," which I thought was the most beautiful music I had ever seen. At about this time, too, I came to know some of the Beethoven sonatas, which my father brought back from his European trip in 1867. They made a deep impression on me. How well I remember my delight when this new world of great music was revealed to me! And it was the same later with Wagner and Brahms. In the last sixty years many new valuations have been made: Bach has come to be understood a little as he really is, a living force and not merely a name. Most of Haydn and Mozart, on the other hand, have been discarded, while we no longer have the foolish idea that every note written by Beethoven was pure gold. The day has gone by when it seemed natural to have all his symphonies in one season of the symphony concerts, as was the case in the eighties. Much of the music of that period is coming to be interesting only in the way that Fielding and Miss Austen are interesting. We now know that there are commonplace songs of Schubert and Schumann, but time can never dim such works as the "Winterreise," the "Dichter-liebe," and their many other beautiful songs. Most of Mendelssohn and Liszt have disappeared, Chopin being the only one of the group to grow in stature (as later Brahms).

At that time Dwight's *Journal of Music* was a weekly visitor (in exchange for my father's paper, the *Salem Gazette*), and I cannot be too grateful for its influence on my taste and knowledge. Dwight (a retired parson) was not a thoroughly educated musician but a man of sensibility and cultivation, with a sincere appreciation of what was best in music, and with the advantage of having as counselor Otto Dresel. Dresel was a man of thorough knowledge, real talent in composition, a pianist of exquisite taste and feeling, profound convictions as to what was best and what was negligible, and consequently with pretty strong prejudices, as later against Brahms and Wagner (He used to say that he would not sleep in the same room with a Wagner score). Dresel in after years was to be for me an inspiration.

In 1869 Frank H. Lee (son of John C. Lee, brother of Mrs. Endicott Peabody), who was sincerely interested in things musical, imported from England copies of the " Creation," " Messiah," and " Elijah " for the Salem Oratorio Society, which was just being formed, with Zerrahn as conductor. For at that time came the famous Peace Jubilee of Boston, a conception of Pat Gilmore of Gilmore's Band, at which there were thousands of singers from all parts of New England. There was an orchestra of hundreds (Zerrahn conductor) and famous soloists from abroad. I sang in the Salem chorus, and, as one of it, was present at the concerts of this Jubilee, as also at those of its successor in 1872. These Jubilees had much about them that was sensational, as well as much that seems to us today rather naïve; but they had a marked effect in awaking a real interest in good music, for all these choruses that took part perforce became familiar with works such as the " Messiah " and the like. As an instance of the sensational features may be mentioned the punctuation in rhythms afforded by cannon that were fired to emphasize strong accents, and the fifty red-shirted firemen who beat the time on anvils for the " Anvil Chorus " of " Il Trovatore." One charming episode was the conducting by Johann Strauss of his famous waltzes; another was the performance of the foreign bands, Dan Godfrey's " Guards," the " Garde Républicaine," and one of the crack German bands, all of which were superior to our own. One of these Jubilees (I think the second) took place in a specially constructed vast hall near the railroad bridge on Huntington Avenue.

III·THE GAZETTE

AND NOW TO LEAVE MY MUSIC, AND SPEAK OF THE *Salem Gazette* and my father's manner of life. He was part owner and chief editor of this paper (his partner being Nathaniel A. Horton), which was published Tuesday and Friday. Its weekly, the *Essex County Mercury,* edited with special regard to the smaller towns of the county, came out on Wednesdays. Other papers were the *Register,* Mondays and Thursdays, and the *Observer* on Saturdays. They were excellent papers, exerting a real influence, especially my father's, I think, in which the editorials (chiefly his) were able and fearless. It was an illustration of the advantage, to a newspaper, of the editors being owners. The *Springfield Republican* is the strongest survivor of this group of newspapers. My father foresaw the day when the then type of paper would have to give way to the daily, and about 1880 wished to change the *Gazette* in this way, offering to stand the necessarily large expenses of the first years. But Horton, in poor health, had not the courage nor perhaps the strength to go in for this, so that very shortly they had the annoyance of the birth of the daily *Salem News,* which a few years later forced the proprietors

[26]

of the *Gazette* to turn it into a daily. But it was too late: in a precarious way the *Gazette* lived on a few years longer, and then expired. I am glad that my father's death in 1894 prevented his knowing this pathetic ending of a fine old newspaper that had lived since 1765.

There was one odd custom in those days — that of the boys who " carried " the paper, appearing New Year's Day at the houses of subscribers with an " Address," usually in poetry, and receiving a small gratuity therefor. Hawthorne, by the way, wrote one of these addresses (which, no doubt, is to be found at the Essex Institute).

My father's routine was a fixed one: after breakfast a walk down town to the office (usually stopping at the market in Derby Square) — back to dinner — then to the office again for the afternoon; back again after supper (till nine o'clock), except Tuesday and Friday, the days of publication. Tuesday evenings there was always a call on " Aunt Nancy" Cole; Sundays nearly always a good walk with me, often in the pastures, and not seldom to the cemetery at Harmony Grove. I look back and realize how little I understood of my father's solitary life for almost forty years. If we only had in early youth something of the sympathy and understanding that comes to us later! There was no eight-hour day for my father.

[27]

How well I remember the smell of that ramshackle, dusty old printing office in Essex Street, up two very steep flights! They had at that time only hand presses for printing, a large ball of some soft substance (probably cloth) being wet with ink from time to time and rubbed over the type, which was of course set by hand. This printing must have been a tedious process.

The most conspicuous instance of the influence of the *Gazette* was concerned with the well-known Ben Butler, who had managed to get himself elected as a Republican in the Essex district. My father's paper was the only one which had the courage and honesty to oppose and expose him (all the Boston papers had dutifully " come to heel "). But before long my father and Horton had the satisfaction of seeing the example of the *Gazette* followed by the others, and Butler really driven out of the Republican party. He then turned Democrat. I was sometimes present at political meetings with Mr. Horton, who reported them for the paper. I remember the campaign of Butler against Dana (father of my classmate). For some time (after having abandoned my plan of being a railroad engineer) I expected eventually to succeed my father as editor. Indeed, I did not think of music as a profession until after leaving college.

IV · COLLEGE

AND NOW FOR HARVARD. ENTERING IN JUNE, 1870, without conditions, I had my room (with Fenollosa as chum) in the freshman year in College House; and during the three following years I roomed alone at 49 Grays. None of the buildings had modern conveniences, and we certainly lived plainly. I ate at " Commons," a wooden building near the corner of Kirkland Street and North Avenue, which had formerly been the station for a small local railway to Boston, I believe. Board was about four dollars a week. When sweet potatoes were plenty they appeared at about every meal. Beef stew was a staple. And we often muttered among ourselves, rather unreasonably, at the monotony, not realizing then what inexpensive board had to be like. The old, rough custom of throwing pieces of bread from one table to another (even, I fear, sometimes crockery, spoons, and so forth) still existed; and we were an ill-mannered lot, no doubt. For the last two years I was at a club table, which was fairly good, at six dollars a week, and more pleasant. My grandfather, Daniel A. White (Class of 1817), had been one of the founders of the Pudding,[1] but in my junior year, with Merwin, Fenollosa, and others, I went into the Pi Eta [2] in the first ten. We gave plays, musical and otherwise, in which, naturally, I was the musical factor. By the way, Charles A. Macintosh of the Pi Eta was a good actor and a great friend of Cheever Goodwin, who lived in my entry in Grays, so that later I was much with them and with **Ed Rice** (author of " Evangeline," who married the daughter of Isaac Rich, later the manager of the Hollis Street Theater). We three, with others, did a little barnstorming in some theatrical shows in the neighboring towns (I guess about the year 1875), I performing on the piano under the name of Ernest Fabian. I remember one particular evening at Allston (why, I don't know).

A very delightful experience was my being leader of the Glee Club in the last two years. The fellows were a fine lot: Lithgow Devens, Vin Bowditch, Emor Harding, Dick Dana, John Farlow, Ernest Fenollosa, and others, our number being between sixteen and twenty. The programs were (as I can see by one which is in my scrap-book) really good, though not " high-brow " — far bett r than they became later, from 1885 until the present kind of Glee Club came

---

[1] Hasty Pudding Club.
[2] Another club at Harvard.

into existence through Davison.[3] Then (as now in an ambitious way) we went out of town in addition to the Cambridge and Boston concerts, e. g. to New Bedford, Salem, Concord (Mass.), and even Portland. I regret to say that the more alcoholic the town, the better its standing with us, New Bedford being an especial favorite for that reason. At Salem we naturally " serenaded " at Fenollosa's house. But as there was nothing to drink there — only ice-cream and the like — I fear that we rather rudely hastened our departure to the house of the father of Chud Tuckerman (who was an associate member of the Club), where we knew that there were drinks. This was rather different from the present Glee Club, with its strict rules and training. Occasionally we went off with the Pierian Sodality. After a concert in Portland I remember there was dancing, for which the Pierian played, while we sang at least one waltz, I shall probably never feel as proud as when, at that concert, Devens warbled " Seeing Nellie Home " in the most fetching manner, doing great execution among the girls, while I played the most fascinating accompaniments I could think up. At that concert I probably gave them either Liszt's " Rigoletto " or Raff's " Polka de la Reine," battle-horses of mine. At that

[3] Professor Archibald T. Davison, who converted the Glee Club into a men's choral society after he became its Director in 1912.

time " La Fille de Madame Angot " was the rage, while the little pieces of Grieg had just been published. 49 Grays was a rendezvous for those who loved music.

For our Class Day, Fenollosa was poet and Dick Dana orator. The poem was a remarkable production for a youngster, and one remembered for years afterward. I was chorister (feeling very important in the march round the Tree, on which was hung the wreath to be struggled for) , and I wrote a Class song to words by Dole.[4] I was, by the way, a member of the Phi Beta Kappa. That is, on the whole, I had good marks. But I look back to but little real teaching; nor do I seem to remember many who made us vitally interested in really learning, in acquiring the ability to think. One of the valuable things I got was at least some knowledge of German. Having worked out the first year's course by myself one summer, I was able to go into the more advanced reading. For that, and for what knowledge of French I possess (one thing which I did get at " Daddy " Waters') , I have always been thankful. The elective system was just beginning at this time.

I was unwise enough not to work at piano-playing in college, not realizing my inadequacy because I read rapidly and with understanding. But I did take

4 Nathan Haskell Dole.

Prof. John Knowles Paine's courses, and I owe him a great deal. In later years I came to know him intimately and to be fond of him. He was not one of the born teachers, but certainly he could give generously. Looking back at some of the fugues, etc., of which I have preserved the manuscripts, I am surprised to find how good the result of our work was. His influence was always for what was strong and good in music. After graduation I studied with him for another year, receiving in 1875 the degree of A.M. for work in music, the first time it was ever given in this country for excellence in this subject.

V · The Organ

And so I left Cambridge, going back to salem to live, for a while at least. By my recollection I expected to go to St. Mark's School in Southboro, as successor in Latin and music (organist, etc.) to Warren A. Locke (of 1869), who was just going abroad to finish his musical studies. After a year or so of this I was to go to the Law School. But Fate stepped in, and the profession of the law has escaped one rather inefficient exponent. For I am confident that I was meant to do just what I have done.

Wishing to use the summer of 1874 to advantage, I decided to learn something about the organ, and to go to B. J. Lang, who had heard me play the piano, and who was a Salem boy like myself (this last point decided me, queerly enough). And so every week I went to Boston for my lesson with him at Dr. E. E. Hale's church, at that time on Union Park Street, where the music was famous. The singers there were Mrs. Julia Houston West, Mrs. Rametti, William and John Winch. Lang was remarkably gifted as an organist, excelling in improvising. I have never heard any church service with a quartet choir to equal the sort of thing they gave you at Sunday afternoon Vespers, at which I was a constant attendant from now on. Lang was able to give me a few foundation-principles on which to build, which in later years I found to cover the ground perfectly. His ideas were in advance of what was common in this country then. Looking back at what I accomplished that summer, I see that it was something unusual. In later years I had reason to regret not having studied longer and more thoroughly; for though even in recitals I think my musical side carried me through, I never felt wholly secure technically. But I might as well confess now, as at any time, that as to *practising* at either piano or organ I have not a creditable record. First, things came too easily. Second, I had no real standard of performance, as none of us had until we were taught by Kneisel, Gericke, and others later. And third, it is, in fact, only in these last twenty years that I have come to the point of knowing that, whether we can attain it or not, our goal should be perfection.

To complete the story of the organist part of my life. In 1876, through Lang (whose influence in the way of putting pupils ahead, having them play in public, and in finding church positions, etc., was remarkable, and today could not be duplicated, even by as clever a person as he), I got the organ position at the Church of the Disciples, then on Warren Avenue. James Freeman Clarke, an unusual man, was minister, and his sermons (printed weekly in the *Saturday Evening Gazette*) were well worth hearing. Largely through his influence the church was a place that meant much to its people, who, by the way, were kind and hospitable to me. All that I had to do was voluntaries and hymns, so that it was an easy, gradual, and efficient preparation for what was to follow. I enjoyed my musical life there. Later the church moved over to Jersey Street, where it is now.[1] Twenty-five years later I played (as did also Albert Snow and Frank Lynes, the organist of the church at the time) at the dedication of their new organ.

In 1878 I was offered the position in the First Church, and began there in October, remaining for thirty-two years. There had been a new deal all round, and we had a choir of whom three, as well as myself, were twenty-five years old, Fessenden,[2] the tenor, being the only one older. It was a remarkably good quartet as to voices and musical ability, and very pleasant on the personal side. Dr. James C. White, then living in Park Square, was chairman of the committee, and very interested in the work. Soon after our beginning he had us all to dinner at his house, as to which I remember only a remarkable Rhine wine

---

[1] More recently the church has been joined with the First Church (Unitarian) of Boston at Marlborough and Berkeley Streets.

[2] William H. Fessenden, a charming tenor and good musician, later a popular member of the " Bostonians."

(just as of William Everett's hospitality, in my sopho-
more year, do I cherish the recollection of a certain
Stein-wein; for Everett, though forbidding a cigarette
in his house, was a connoisseur of wines) . The min-
isters of the church during my stay were Dr. Rufus
Ellis; Stopford Brooke, who later dropped the
" Rev." when he went back to England, after marry-
ing Helen Ellis (a relative of some sort to Rufus
Ellis) ; James Eells, and Charles Edwards Park, the
present occupant of the pulpit. With all of these my
relations were most pleasant and helpful. The service
of the church was practically the modified one of
King's Chapel. But by degrees one minister after
another made amputations and changes in it, so that
finally the Te Deum, etc., was dropped, and the present form came to be used. As to this latter, it pleases
me that a set of responses which I wrote at Dr. Park's
suggestion are still used every Sunday, twenty years
after they were written in 1905.

We had at first morning and afternoon services,
but after a while stopped the latter. The position was
thus an easy one, even with the Thursday afternoon
short service (later) , of which half was a recital by
the organist. I also gave a few regular organ recitals
during my incumbency. The work was very enjoya-
ble indeed. As a church organist I was more of a success than in concert; for I have not the temperament

for public playing of either organ or piano. Naturally I was led to the composition of a good many anthems, as well as some organ pieces. Of the anthems the only one to be well known is " Still, Still with Thee," oddly enough one of the most difficult. I have always been happy that Guilmant, in two of his tours, used compositions of mine, as did Bonnet later, quite out of whole cloth. There were in the thirty-two years not a few changes in the choir. Miss Louise Gage was succeeded by Mrs. Humphrey-Allen, Mrs. Hascall, Mrs. Dunton Wood, Mrs. Galvin, and others; and Mrs. Jeanette Noyes was followed by Lillian Carllsmith, Anna Miller Wood, and others. George J. Parker, William Dunham, and Walton L. Crocker, all familiar names, were among our tenors, while Clarence Hay, who antedated me by a year, remained as bass several years after I left.

In 1910, after the many years of happy service, one of those decisions was made that seem to come at the appointed time in one's life, that of retiring from church work. The organ was perhaps secondary to composition and pianoforte teaching when activities came to be lessened. Of course I missed the pleasant associations and my organ; and today, fifteen years later, I still feel the loss. Yet I can see that the sacrifice had to be made. When I left them the church people were generous to me in their kind words, and gave me besides a handsome sum of money. A year or two later I gave the money to Courtenay Pollock for one of his beautiful portrait busts, of myself. About a year after my leaving, the quartet was given up and a chorus choir instituted — I feel now to the advantage of the service. At the time, from old associations, I naturally wished the old arrangement to be retained. For the first part of my incumbency, we had a German organ (the builder being the same as of the famous Music Hall organ) at the chancel end of the church. It was, however, not well adapted to use with a quartet; and in 1903 Mrs. Jacob C. Rogers gave us a beautiful organ in memory of her husband, a member of my music committee for some years. It was placed in the gallery, and the music gained greatly through this change.

At about 1900 the New England chapter of the American Guild of Organists (of which I had been a founder) was formed. George A. Burdett, who became Dean, made a record for efficiency at a very important time. In 1909–1912 I was made honorary president of the Guild, in succession to Dudley Buck, Samuel P. Warren and Horatio Parker. This I have always felt to be a real distinction.

VI·THE PIANO

As I am coming to the piano now, it is perhaps not a bad time to speak of concerts, etc., at that period (the 1870's). Soon after I began musical work in Boston, I was made one of the committee that managed the concerts of the Harvard Musical Association, which were then approaching their end. At first they had been very successful, and had accumulated a fund which had carried them through the lean years (of which the last was 1881). Programs were conservative to be sure, but Lang, Apthorp, and I managed to have introduced a good deal that was new. Theodore Thomas, with more attractive programs and a far better orchestra, had shown us what first-rate playing really was. The Thomas concerts, then, were dangerous for the H. M. A. A rival orchestra, the Philharmonic, did us no good. But the *coup de grâce* after a final year (in which the concerts were held in the Boston Museum) was given by the Symphony Orchestra founded by H. L. Higginson, with Henschel as conductor. As a matter of record let me just run over the names of the conductors: Georg [1] Henschel, Wil-

[1] Some years later, while living in England, where he remained until his death in 1934, Henschel changed his first name to George. He was knighted in 1914.

helm Gericke, Arthur Nikisch, Emil Paur, Wilhelm
Gericke (again), Karl Muck, Max Fiedler, Muck
(again), Rabaud, Monteux, Koussevitzky. This constant change of conductors (in contrast with Chicago,
where in thirty-five years there have been but two,
Thomas and Stock) seems to me not to have been
fortunate. Theodore Thomas, who showed us here
for the first time what fine orchestral playing was, and
was looked up to by those who were in the musical
life of the next twenty years (1880–1900) as the ideal
conductor, was offered the post by Higginson when
Nikisch's engagement came to a sudden and unfortunate end.[2] But he refused, although he had (as he
said to some of us) looked forward to conducting the
Boston orchestra as the crown of his career. He refused simply because, although the Chicago orchestra
was in a rickety condition (in 1894), he felt that his
backers there had been so loyal, and his obligation
to the orchestra was so imperative, that his duty lay
there. Here was a fine example of character, empha-

---

[2] And, by first-hand testimony, dramatic. Both Nikisch and Higginson were present at a reception in the house of Mrs. Montgomery Sears
toward the close of the conductor's fourth season in Boston. Nikisch had
mentioned casually to a little group that he had received an offer from
the Royal Opera at Budapesth, and that he didn't know how to answer
— all said with the air of one who is looking for a polite and tactful way
to refuse. Higginson, standing by and overhearing Nikisch's remarks,
turned to him and said, " I think I should accept if I were you." Nikisch
was probably as surprised as anyone present. There had evidently been
no previous intimation that the differences between the conductor and
the orchestra's founder were too serious to be resolved amicably.

sized by the fact that Thomas never made any talk about it, so that only half a dozen people in Chicago and a few in Boston (of whom I was one) knew about it at the time.

In going to Lang in 1874 for organ lessons, I had no intention of more than just that. Little did I think that I was to find in them later the happiest of pursuits. But as I grew more interested that summer, and was much encouraged as to a musical career by Lang, I changed my plans entirely in October, and decided to begin piano lessons with Lang seriously. I was a tough case to start with. With much natural ability at the keyboard, some experience, and a good deal of musical knowledge to back all of this, I only played notes, without sensitiveness or real musical feeling (like many of my pupils since), and also played by sheer effort and will-power, being stiffer and less comfortable muscularly than any pupil I've ever had. So that it was long before I got into any kind of shape. Moreover, it was a great many years before I had real feeling for what is called " touch." I saw Dresel, for example, with an exquisite feeling for lovely tone and expression in playing, and admired his results, without having sense to find out how he got them; and today look back with regret to the many years in which what is now to me the best side of playing was a secret. I was so able in some ways as to be obstinate

in others, and was too well satisfied with my unsympathetic playing. On the intellectual side it was really
good, but I was blind to the fact that I was wanting in
the sensuous, beautiful element in piano playing, with
little feeling for quality in tone and finesse in phrasing. Lang warned me against the " academic," while
Philip Hale's expression, " ligneous touch," should
have made me think. The truth is that I was not one
of those who have the instinct that leads them to de-
mand beauty as well as competence. This, no doubt,
was one of the reasons why I was not meant to be a
concert player. I was also cursed with too great facil-
ity, and had little idea of what concentrated,
thorough practice is. Besides all this, the standard as
to all kinds of performance, in piano playing, violin,
organ, chamber music, and orchestra, was not exact-
ing. Lang had such vogue and influence as to be able
to help his pupils by recommending them as teachers, so that I was soon busy with lessons. Customs
were different in those days, and rates for teaching
were low as compared with now, my terms being
forty dollars a quarter (twenty lessons) when once a
week, fifty dollars when twice, while I went a good
deal to the houses. Until 1915, when I gave up much
of my work, I had always had a large number of pupils from outside of Boston, a good proportion of
them being teachers themselves.

[43]

My first recital, in 1876, which I played with the music before me (for I had not been forced to memorize), was followed, until about 1895, by others in Boston and elsewhere, while several times I made little trips of a week or so for concerts in New York, Michigan, etc., from 1884 until 1909. In 1876 I assisted at two of Lang's concerts in Boston, playing with him for the first time in this country the (then new) St. Saëns Variations for two pianos. In these concerts a wonderful young girl, Lillian Bailey, afterwards Mrs. Georg Henschel, made her first appearance: a lovely voice and most beautiful singing — one of the finest artists I have known. She, her mother, brother, and uncle (Charles R. Hayden), lived at the top of Hotel Pelham (where the Little Building now stands), and I was a frequent visitor, making much music there with her. These were the days when St. Saëns' music came to us as a stunning novelty, when (1875) we had the first (MS.) performance by Von Bülow of the Tschaikowsky Concerto with Lang conducting (what a sensation it was!); when the new Grieg Concerto fascinated every one, and when some of us went over to Bayreuth in 1876 to the first performances of the " Niebelungen Ring." It was a time when I used to listen with delight to the Theodore Thomas orchestra, admiring him from a distance and little thinking that twenty years later I should know the great man well, and be honored by his playing of my compositions (I still have the telegrams and letters that he sent after such performances). Lang was a musician of great gifts and very versatile; a composer of originality, who would have been considered one of our leading men had he published, and a teacher of incredible activity (when I knew him he was giving regularly lessons from 8.30 to 6). As conductor of the Apollo Club and the Cecilia Society, he brought out an extraordinary number of important works, while as pianist he performed for the first time most of the novelties that came along from 1870 to 1900; for he was eager to know and to show others new and significant developments in music. The most striking individual undertakings were his concert performances of Berlioz' "Damnation de Faust" and of "Parsifal."

In the wonderful days of the Kneisel Quartet (say, 1890 to 1910) I played with it a good many times, chiefly at first performances of my own compositions. Not only had I the honor and happiness of having a hearing for my Violin Sonata, Piano Trio in B-flat, Piano Quartet and Quintet, and String Quartet, but also learned much from Kneisel through his suggestions as to practical points in composition, and I became aware of a different and higher standard of performance through my work with him in rehearsal.

All this has been a matter for deep gratitude; and I fancy that Parker, Chadwick, Mrs. Beach, Helen Hopekirk, and other composers would tell the same story. When Kneisel died, in 1925, the grief was accompanied by the old feeling of thankfulness and a never-to-be-forgotten appreciation of his encouragement.

To return to the piano: In 1883, when we were at Neuilly for the summer (and a happy summer it was!), I had a few lessons on his own compositions with Stephen Heller. The remembrance of the experience is dear to me. He was a man of great charm and simplicity (like his music), who, though not interesting himself much on the technical side of playing, yet gave me some of the most valuable hints that I ever had. The next year, 1884, he was in real want, and I was able to collect a little money to send to the fund being raised by Charles Hallé. I mention this to show the iniquity of our copyright laws at that time; for if he had received from his Studies alone what he would now, he could have ended his days in ease.

Then later, in 1888, having corresponded with Leschetizky as to the possibility of some lessons from him, I stopped at Ischl to see him on my way back from Vienna, where I had been visiting the Wilsons (Madame Hopekirk and her husband), whom I had known in Madame Hopekirk's visits to Boston for concerts. Into a few days many things had been crowded, and I had a delightful stay with them. She had been a pupil of Leschetizky after her American visit. And as both husband and wife were charming people, they had become intimate friends with him. I had not expected any difficulty as to working with him, from what he had written, and in fact had already arranged for a piano to be sent to my lodgings. But although he was cordial, played to me and had me play to him, he refused to give any lessons while on his vacation. Within a few weeks I was to be thankful for this instead of disappointed, as will be seen later. On leaving Ischl I made a détour, to be a day at Wiesbaden, in order to meet MacDowell and Templeton Strong, in whose compositions some of us had become interested. From there to Paris. In the train from Cologne to Paris there was an unpleasant experience. Two soldiers in the compartment, somewhat drunk, terrorized the others who were in it — an incident which came back vividly to the mind thirty years later, at the time of the great war. From Paris I journeyed to Dinan, where my wife and daughter had gone to visit (Château de Grand Cour). We used to go into the town to the bathing establishment, where one saw a donkey treading a circular path to pump the water, and a raven heartening him with his cries. Leaving Dinan, we went to Dinard by a little steamer that ran down the river Rance, a picturesque voyage. After some delightful days at Dinard, with various excursions to St. Lunaire, St. Briac, St. Malo and Mont St. Michel, we took the boat for Jersey, where I had reason to be glad that my lessons with Leschetizky had come to naught, for the little daughter came down with typhoid on the day of our arrival. And at St. Helier's we remained for nearly a month, my wife taking care of her in the day, and I at night. As soon as it was safe we took the steamer for England. I left for home within a week or so, and they remained until it was prudent for them to follow. If, however, I could have had those lessons my future piano playing would have been far better.

Today I realize that concert-playing should be done only by those who are fitted for it not alone by ability, but by the inborn natural feeling for it. But this I did not then realize, while it seemed then advisable to play in concert for one's reputation (as indeed is the case today). It is also a natural ambition, that of being a real " pianist," just as many of us have wished to become conductors. In each case the desire usually remains unsatisfied, while we end by being teachers. But at one period I played in as many as seventy-five concerts yearly.

THE PIANO

As I have said, I continued to be very busy with lessons until 1915, when, after a bad pneumonia, it was decided that work must be cut in half, and restricted to mornings. My teaching rooms were first at the Chickering Building at 153 Tremont Street, afterwards at 6 Newbury Street, where Lang and a colony of his pupils occupied rooms at the Lang Studios, since 1915 at the house, and in 1921 I began to teach somewhat at the Conservatory, finding it very pleasant there. I can never be too grateful that this work (?) of teaching is today, at seventy-three, more interesting than ever, probably from the fact that results are more satisfying than at any previous time.

VII·Composing

ONE VALUABLE EXPERIENCE FOR A NUMBER OF YEARS
came from my connection with the Music Teachers
National Association (M. T. N. A.), and my attendance to its annual meetings. In 1884 Lang, being invited to attend a meeting of teachers at Cleveland to
organize a teachers society for standardizing instruction, took H. G. Tucker and me along with him. He
did not much fancy the way things were run, or the
people who ran them, and so had no further interest
in the matter; but I felt differently, and went later to
meetings of the M. T. N. A. at Indianapolis, Cleveland, Detroit, Philadelphia, etc. In 1886 there was a
very successful meeting at Boston, the duty of manag-
ing the concert side of it falling to me. Two things of
value came from my interest in this society. First, I
thus became acquainted with most of the best musicians not living in New York or Boston, thereby
much broadening my ideas, and doing away with a
certain provincial conceit that we are apt to have
here. Second, through their concerts came the first
real chance of a hearing of my compositions in large
form. At that time an American writing serious
music was a rare bird, opportunities for a hearing be-

[50]

ing hard to get. To these concerts I thus owe the beginning of what reputation I may have.

In the same way, and to even a greater degree, do I feel my debt to my publisher, Arthur P. Schmidt, who was the first here to bring out the larger works of our composers, beginning this disinterested work with the publication, by subscription, of the Spring Symphony by J. K. Paine. He later followed this with orchestral and chamber music and choral works of Mrs. Beach, Chadwick, Hadley, MacDowell, and others. Of my compositions the first was a Trio in C minor (of which lately another edition has been printed), published in connection with Schott & Co., with their imprint as publishers. This was followed by a Serenade for strings, a Symphonic Prologue, "Francesca da Rimini," a Suite in D minor, a Suite for string orchestra, "Four Character Pieces after Omar Khayyam" (being a transcription from the "Five Poems for Piano"), a Violin Sonata, a Second Trio in A-flat major, a Quartet and a Quintet for violin and strings, a Theme and Variations for strings and a String Quartet, besides short pieces for violin and piano and for 'cello and piano, many songs and other works.

When it is remembered that before Schmidt there had been published in this country no music other than such as was of comparatively small consequence, it is obvious that what he did was of far-reaching importance. As an illustration of the small output of music of the better class fifty years ago, a program of a certain piano recital of that time is excellent. In 1877 Annette Essipoff, a fine pianist, at that time the wife of Leschetizky, was giving concerts here. Her manager thought to stimulate interest by a recital of American music, the program of which is a curiosity, being made up of pieces by William Mason, John K. Paine, and Gottschalk (as the most important number), and made of a reasonable length by the inclusion of transcriptions from European composers by Perabo and others. At the time I had just finished writing my first piano pieces, and left the MS. of one of them (a Gavotte, rather poor stuff) at the office of the hotel where Essipoff was staying. I had the delight later of hearing it played at this concert spoken of. The sensation of hearing a public performance of one's work, for the first time, can be imagined.

1873 is the date of my first hearing of one of the great players, Rubinstein. I was too green really to appreciate him as I should today; but even then it was a tremendous experience. I remember just how he played certain phrases (e. g., in the Chopin Fantaisie in F minor), and the loveliness and variety of his tone. At that time we believed that " touch " was a gift of the Gods, the secret of which could not be learned by common folk. Now the matter has been analyzed and standardized. We know that certain procedures produce certain results. The piano teaching of those days seems, looking back, to have been mainly unintelligent. Doubtless our greater knowledge is responsible for the higher standard of today. In 1875 von Bülow came, and again a few years later. Since 1900 the number of big players who have visited us has increased year by year until, after the war in 1918, we had here a large majority of the best players in the world, a great stimulation to our musical life.

In 1893 Theodore Thomas invited Chadwick, Whiting, and me to the Chicago Exposition, and gave my Serenade for string orchestra in one of his programs; and I played my Piano Quartet with the Kneisels, a wonderful experience, most of all because it brought me Thomas's friendship. The weather (in May) was very raw (Chicago at its worst), and the plastered walls of the buildings were not yet dry. At a performance of the " Creation " Thomas had on a heavy coat and hat, Nordica a fur coat, and the audience was dismissed at the end of the second part. Later, in 1899, I had another good time at the M. T. N. A. meeting at Cincinnati, where I played my Piano Quintet, and Whiting his Fantaisie with orchestra. In 1913 the annual meeting of the Institute of Arts and Letters was at Chicago. Stock, who had just been elected a member, had the idea of a regular concert of the Orchestra at which the program should be made up of compositions by our members. At this I conducted my " Omar Khayyam " Suite, there being also compositions of Chadwick, Kelley, and the MacDowell Concerto (Edith Thompson). About 1905, at the suggestion of Helen Hopekirk, I had scored the " Omar Khayyam " pieces, but not with the expectation of ever hearing them, — simply for practice. I sent them to Stock, who liked them well enough to play them two successive years. Later Fiedler took them up; and their success was such that I published them, with the result that they turned out to be my most successful work for orchestra, and were played practically everywhere. In the early days of the Boston Symphony Orchestra (1890–1905), composers frequently conducted their own works. The Orchestra was kind to those of us who were without experience, and it was good fun for us. Since then, however, the practice has been abandoned.

In the early nineties there were a number of us in Boston writing music more or less worth while, some of which has lived (e.g., Parker's " Hora Novissima," Chadwick's " Melpomene "). They

were Chadwick, Horatio Parker, Whiting, Mac-
Dowell, Nevin, John Paine, J. C. D. Parker, Mrs.
Beach, Margaret Ruthven Lang, Mrs. H. M. Rogers;
Converse and Hadley were to come a little later.
Parker was still in Boston weekly as organist of
Trinity Church, and Whiting had not yet gone to
New York. These two, with Chadwick and me, used
sometimes to meet at the St. Botolph Club after dinner. We allowed ourselves frank discussion and the
most out-spoken criticism I have ever heard. I got no
end of good from it. As an example of what a few
words can do in the way of opening one's eyes, I remember Parker saying, after I had ended the playing
through of a movement from my orchestra Suite,
" All in D minor, isn't it? " And that was the trouble;
easily remedied by the simple alteration of some authentic cadences to deceptive ones. This pleasant
association came to an end when Whiting went to
New York, and Parker to New Haven as Professor at
Yale.

It was not until 1877 that I attempted to write real
music. I was late in this respect in comparison with
Chadwick, Parker, and MacDowell; and of course I
lacked their training. My first published music was
three pieces for 'cello (reminiscent and rather of a
stencil pattern, but melodious) , which I played with
Wulf Fries a good deal. This, as well as the three pi-

ano pieces referred to before, was published by Cranz
of Hamburg, for whom Schmidt was agent, as he was
for Litolff. These pieces are all commonplace, but
their composition gave me encouragement; and from
that time until a few years ago I was very busy indeed
putting notes on paper. The most significant things
of this period are the first Trio (finished the summer
we were at Neuilly, in 1883, and played from MS. in
one of my own chamber concerts), the little Serenade
for strings, and an Overture, " In the Mountains."
The latter two were produced by Gericke with the
Boston Symphony Orchestra (at about the time
when he brought out Chadwick's " Melpomene,"
that proved so successful). Though I knew little
about orchestration, the Overture is effective, if old-
fashioned; and it is singular that, in spite of my not
playing any stringed instrument, nor indeed knowing in detail about the technique of even the violin,
everything for strings has been practical and grateful.
Much of my early reputation came from the Overture and from this Trio, which forty years afterwards
is still sometimes on programs. At about this time
came a setting of an extract from " Hiawatha "
(Apollo Club, Boston) with orchestra, which is today still going strong, while the " Bedouin Song " for
men's voices (afterwards arranged for mixed voices)
is probably the most successful piece of the sort

[56]

written by an American (1892). A Violin Sonata
(1890), dedicated to Kneisel, has had an unusual
number of concert performances, as has also a
Quartet for piano and strings in C major (written at
the Alhambra, Mrs. Gardner's cottage at Pride's
Crossing, in 1891). This last I have probably played
myself in at least forty concerts. In 1884 my first song,
" Go, Lovely Rose," written for Mrs. Henschel, was
published, to be followed by probably one hundred
twenty-five others. " I'm Wearing Awa'," written one
Sunday morning before going to church, and the
" Irish Folk Song," written to be sung at a reception
given to Gilbert Parker, have been the most successful, still selling after thirty-five years. As a musician I
prefer many of my later ones as being more original
and of greater interest harmonically. As to this last
point, my influences from the beginning, as well as
my predilection, were ultra-conservative: as a boy,
General Oliver, later Emery and Paine, later still
Dresel were my mentors; and I formed myself, so to
speak, on Mendelssohn (having none the less a love
for Schumann and Chopin). Consecutive fifths, even
cross-relations, were anathema to my teachers and
to me. My harmony was correct but with little variety, the structure of my pieces conventional; and it
was only much later that I absorbed harmonic finesse
and became sensitive to it. Somehow, although

[57]

deeply moved by Wagner, I did not have sense enough for a long time to learn from his music, and was late in appreciating the early Debussy. The idea that certain things simply must not be had become too thoroughly ingrained.

Later, 1894–1897, came a Suite for orchestra (Boston Symphony Orchestra with Paur, 1896), which was completed at Hythe, England, in 1895, and was only fairly successful, but with two really good movements; and a Quintet for piano and strings. In 1897, at Meudon, there was a very fruitful summer (something like the one at Hull in 1890) as to songs and piano pieces, while the next summer is marked by the " Five Poems after Omar Khayyam," my best and most successful piano pieces. We were in Dedham, and enjoying our first summer in this town. In 1900–1915 the most successful things were an Organ Suite; the little " Twenty Preludes " for piano; half a dozen organ pieces written after returning from California; a second Trio, less conventional and of greater interest harmonically and structurally than the one of twenty-five years before, but perhaps not so fresh; several violin pieces (of which the Ballade is the best) ; a Suite for string orchestra (Boston Symphony Orchestra with Fiedler, Monteux, and Koussevitzky) , of the fugue of which I'm rather proud; and an orchestral version of the " Omar Khayyam " piano pieces (one of which, by the way, has been played not a little by Sousa's Band) . Since 1915 less and less writing, but still there are a few small things, such as the " Night Piece " for flute and strings, and a few of my best songs: " Tranquillity," " Lilac Time," " Lake Isle of Innisfree," and " Three Songs, 1914–1918." With some of the music contained in the bound volumes of my compositions I am even today satisfied; with more of it I'm not. This is the common lot of all composers, and I have not been perhaps so great a sinner as some. We are absorbed at the moment in the work we are doing, but lose interest in it after its completion, and it is hard for the author to estimate real values. As a result, practically all composers have left behind them too much that was published, instead of being torn up after the writing. Besides this, as one grows older, and has ac-quired greater technical mastery, it is natural for a composer, writer, or painter to keep on producing long after he has said all that he had in him. In my time Saint-Saëns was a conspicuous example of this.

VIII·TRAVELS

AMONG THE THINGS THAT STAND OUT MOST CLEARLY in memory are the European experiences and the visit to California. In 1876 came the first European trip. Lang having been a friend of the Wagners, and thereby having an additional reason to be interested in anything to do with them, had been in a way the Boston representative of the Wagner cult. So that this year, as the first performances of the " Ring des Nibelungen " were to take place at Bayreuth in August, he was, of course, to be there with his wife, and was so good as to let the H. G. Tuckers, newly married, and myself go along. There were several other groups of Bostonians who went over chiefly on account of the Bayreuth production.

The month before sailing, my brother and I had been at the Philadelphia Exposition. For the day of the opening exercises Paine and Dudley Buck wrote music (as Paine and Chadwick did for the Chicago exposition seventeen years later) , while Wagner composed his " Centennial March," receiving for it $5000. This March is the weakest of his mature compositions, and was a disappointment, probably most

[60]

of all to Theodore Thomas, through whom Wagner was commissioned to write it.

To me, in this first European experience, all was new and exciting: the first sight of the Irish coast after eight days of water; Liverpool, with its docks and buildings so different from ours; the Northwestern Hotel, with its women clerks and the service so unlike our own. After dinner I went into the station (of which the hotel is a part) to see the locomotives and cars, which I had always heard about (how odd they did look that first time!). And the journey next day to London was a succession of delights: the thatched cottages, the trim look of the railway with its hedges, and the well-cared for appearance of the farms, etc., as we went swiftly along. And then, at London, the hansom cabs which took us through places so familiar from our reading, from Euston to Piccadilly; it was an enchanted day. After a night at the old-fashioned Bath Hotel at the corner of Arlington Street (where I learned that one must order dropped eggs an hour before), we took lodgings at No. 13 of the same street, and I had another experience of something known to me only through Thackeray. These same lodgings were my headquarters later, in 1876 and 1879, as also in 1883 with my wife and daughter. I was introduced by Lang to Schott & Company, the music publishers of 156 Regent Street, and there bought copies of the new Wagner works. Lang, by the way, got hold of an advance copy of the English translation of the libretto, which was passed about from one to another of the Bostonians when we got to Bayreuth. There was but the one copy, so that no one was allowed to have it for more than a day. As today I look over these volumes bought in London fifty years ago, I see how little we then realized that Wagner was the strongest musical influence of these fifty years, 1850–1900, and now know that he was the greatest harmonic discoverer since Bach (even granting that he owed much of this to Liszt) .

In London I made the acquaintance of Randegger, who was to be a delightful friend as long as he lived; and, on our return from the continent, of Korbay, the attractive and talented Hungarian singer. After London came Paris, which in later years I came to love, especially the environs. From there we went via Neufchâtel, Lucerne, Berne, Nuremberg (at that time a small, compact old town, where one might expect to meet a Meistersinger coming round any corner) , to Bayreuth. We arrived two weeks before the performances — fortunately, since we were now informed that there was to be a sort of dress rehearsal of the four operas on the week preceding the date scheduled. And so, not only did I hear the series expected (and paid for at the rate of twenty-five dollars a night) , but also the preliminary performances. We got rooms for a few days at the Hotel Sonne, a typical old-fashioned German hotel, which was to become familiar to so many Americans. These rooms, however, were reserved for some Rothschilds, at whose arrival we had to go to lodgings on the outskirts of the town, at the end of the Rennweg (the main street) .

Besides our party of five, there were opera singers in the house, big women with big voices. At that time the town had not learned the demands made by the floods of visitors that poured into it, and it was overcrowded. In fact, some people preferred to live in Nuremberg, and take the railway journey to and fro, — or indeed perhaps had to, — and the food supply was inadequate. As an unattached man I could wander about and find restaurants where one could get enough to eat, but I fear the Langs had short commons. On the other hand, I naturally came last when it was a question of rooms. My sleeping place was really a sort of large closet, and the bed consisted of bedding laid on some wooden planks supported by large logs. This was the least luxurious experience in the way of rooms that I ever had, the only similar one being that of sleeping in a bath-tub in Munich, when the town was overcrowded.

Bayreuth was full of interesting people: barons,

[63]

countesses, etc. by the score. The Emperor William used to drive past our house in his carriage with outriders; and one day at the theatre, turning a corner, I came across Wagner, Liszt, and the King of Bavaria in talk. I was unluckily prevented by illness from going with the Langs to a reception at the Wagners — especially so, because it was one of the rare times when Liszt played (in later years I have been at these receptions). For the same reason I missed the banquet, at which Wagner made the famous remark as to his giving Germany a " new art." So little did we realize that there would be the many performances during the fifty years since then that, as the train on which we were leaving (a few days after the banquet) rounded a curve which hid the Theatre from us, Lang said to me, as I was leaning out of the window, " You are taking your last look at that."

In returning to England we stopped at Mainz, where I went to Schott's and bought a Wagner transcription as a souvenir. There I had the delight of a first sight of the Rhine, as we took the steamer trip down the river to Cologne. In a fortnight we were back in Boston. Of course this first European experience was an enormous pleasure to me, and the visit to Bayreuth has been one of the high lights of my life. Two years after, my brother was going alone to England to consult Morell McKenzie, the famous throat specialist, and I went a little later to meet him in London and on to Paris, where we found all the world at the Exposition of 1878. There we were at a pension, 130 Rue de Morny (now Rue La Boétie), and had our fill of the exposition; this time I came to know the city a little. After some weeks we went on a trip through the Loire country, then much less visited than now: Chartres, Angers, Le Mans, Tours, and Blois. From there my brother went to Mont Dore for treatment of his throat, and I returned to England. There I saw a good deal of Sidney Holland, whom we had met at our pension in Paris, and one evening we made a tour of the coffee-houses just established in Seven Dials and other quarters, an undertaking in which he was interested. The broad, new avenues of Oxford Street and the Strand had not yet been opened; and these places, where the coffee-houses were, represented some of the worst of London. I saw a number of plays at the Prince of Wales Theatre, a delightful little house, which, although almost in a slum of Soho, was the fashion. It deserved its popularity, for there one saw the most interesting plays, and the pick of England's actors: the Bancrofts, for example, and Ellen Terry, in the " Vicar of Wakefield." The play of the moment was " Diplomacy," in which I remember especially Arthur Cecil, who died too young. This year I really began to feel at home in London and Paris, and not a tourist.

In 1879 came another trip. On the steamer Arthur Astor Carey was a fellow-passenger, and he and I went to the same lodgings that I had had twice before. After a little while in London, Paris once more. Here I was lucky enough to fall in with Frank Chadwick, who was working at painting and living there permanently (as it has turned out even till now, 1926). We were a good deal together, and he introduced me to the restaurant life (something the tourist seldom gets to appreciate). We often went to the Théâtre Français, and of this theatre my strongest recollections are of Bernhardt; Mounet-Sully, in half a dozen performances of " Hernani; " " L'Étrangère " of Dumas (Bernhardt, Croizette, Coquelin) ; " Les Fourchambault " of Augier (Got, Coquelin, Croizette, Reichenberg) ; Delaunay in " Mlle de Belle-Isle " and " Le Gendre de Monsieur Poirier." Since I was lucky in seeing such a group of actors as rarely are found playing together, this summer in Paris has remained in my memory with uncommon distinctness. After a few days in Brussels and in Holland, I returned to England and home. Either this or the previous year I had a sight of English country life through a visit to the Endicott Peabodys (they were then living in England, to return later to Salem), and of an English

[66]

University by a day with Frank Peabody at Trinity College, Cambridge. I also spent a day with the Baileys at Epsom, the remembrance of which is especially pleasant for I first met Georg Henschel, who was teaching Lillian Bailey at this time, and who, as it turned out, was later to marry her. I began then one of those friendships that are really anchors in one's life.

In 1883 (having married Miss Kate Grant Knowlton in 1880) I was again in Paris, with my wife and two-year-old daughter, this time in the suburbs at Neuilly, where we were about two months in a pension five minutes' walk from the Jardin d'Acclimation, and just on the borders of the Bois. It was a happy summer, and confirmed me definitely in my belief that this is the part of the world where one would most wish to live. Here I wrote several piano pieces and finished the Trio, which had been played in MS. at one of my chamber concerts. This performance showed the need of re-writing. I now look back at myself with amusement, the piano part being so absurdly difficult. I was then in the state of mind when one wishes to show all one can do.

After our stay at Neuilly we went to London to the same Arlington Street lodgings. My classmate, Sandy Browne, was in London as legal advisor to the Gilbert & Sullivan operetta undertaking in the States.

He was not only a sparkling companion, but took us often to the Savoy Theatre, and there, annexing the blond and charming Alfred Cellier, the conductor for Gilbert and Sullivan, and later the author of the popular " Dorothy," carried us off for suppers.

Cellier had this story of Sullivan, who had been conductor of the Covent Garden concerts and was suceeded by Cellier. One night he went in with the Prince of Wales (Edward VII) and some friends. The Prince said, " Sullivan, I should like to see you in your old place tonight." Accordingly Sullivan made his way towards the orchestra; and Cellier, see-ing him coming, said to his men, " Mr. Sullivan has been out of this and may not remember to rap for the coda " (the music on the stands was a waltz) . " Don't help him." Sullivan took his place and the waltz went on, the conductor's thoughts being far afield perhaps. He did forget to rap for the coda, and seemed at last to wonder at the length of the number, when the first violin gave the signal and the men went into the coda. But the Prince had noticed, and said, " That was a pretty long waltz, Sullivan."

It has always seemed to me that it was well worth while in travel to get to know the daily life of the peo-ple quite as much as to visit museums and churches. Running about from one place to another rules this out. One must stay long enough in a place to become in a way an inhabitant; while the street life, in which may be included restaurant life, makes the sort of lasting picture that is worth while.

In 1888 we again crossed the water, going after a short stay in London to Paris. I had the interesting experience of going out to St. Germain to dine with Salomé, the chapel organist of La Trinité, where Guilmant played the big organ. In my compartment of the train going back to Paris was a man who, observing some MS. music in my hand, said, " Monsieur is American? " I replied, "Yes, from the United States." " I know the American music, in fact I am an agent for it," said he, " the charming ' Lousiana Lou '! " It turned out that he was an agent for the sort of song that was heard at Olympia and the Folies Bergères, and of course he considered it as the real American music. As a matter of fact " Lousiana Lou " was written by Leslie Stuart, an Englishman.

One event of great interest was the Fourteenth of July celebration. It was incredible, the enormous crowds that filled the Rue de Rivoli and Place Vendôme. I saw the crowd unharnessing the horses and upsetting the carriage of some people who had been so ill-advised as to drive through it. I left Paris to go to Bayreuth for a few days, and from there via Munich to Vienna. I was naturally struck by the extraordinary change in everything that appeared when

[69]

one passed from the German to the Austrian side of
the customs station. Faces, figures, manners, clothes,
uniforms — all so different with the Austrians; wine
instead of beer, and so on.

In June, 1895, abroad again with my family, and
to London, settling in lodgings at Notting Hill near
the Baileys. This time I naturally went out more than
ever before, and the Henschels got our names on several lists: the Felix Moscheles, the Blumenthals, the
Tademas, etc. I was impressed with the magnificence
in entertaining, the large scale of living, and the general feeling of ease everywhere, so changed, alas!
since the war. Through Clayton Johns I had also received a letter from David Bispham (then living in
a charming way at a house in Kensington Gore) , bid-
ding me to a big men's dinner a day or so after my arrival. There I met many musicians, for all the world
was there, Bispham being a man of many friends. I
saw a good deal of him during this stay, and became
intimate with him later when, after being separated
from his wife, he came back to the United States to
live. Henschel gave a dinner for me which was especially interesting; Hubert Parry, Villiers Stanford,
Joseph Barnby and others were there. Of Stanford, I
saw not a little later, and remember well the Sunday
afternoon that he played over his new cantata,
" Phaudrig Crohoore," from MS. after luncheon, — a

composer of great talent, a remarkable teacher, and a charming man. Parry, also at that dinner of Henschel's, impressed me greatly as the finest type of English musician. Mackenzie I came to know later.

The Henschels' large grounds and house in Bedford Gardens (Campden Hill) were beautiful; and they received on Sunday afternoons. There was always music, and one was likely to meet the most worth-while musicians then in town. I have often thought how hard it must have been for him to leave all this after Lillian Henschel's death. He and his wife would sing, and somebody else would play or sing. For instance, one afternoon Mark Hambourg, just back from his study with Leschetitzky, played; and, oddly enough, it was the same week in which I had heard Gabrilowitsch play the Tschaikowsky Concerto in one of the Richter concerts. Since then I have been especially interested in seeing how these two young men, who were then starting their careers, might develop. In the case of the latter, at least, the playing has become more beautiful all the time, and he has also turned out to be a remarkable orchestral conductor. We also saw much of that great actress, our dear friend, Julia Arthur.

This is an opportunity to speak of the pair of artists that we came to know as " the Henschels." Those of us who can now go back thirty years can never forget what were among the most lovely of our musical experiences, those concerts that Georg and Lillian Henschel gave from 1880 to 1900, in which it was difficult to say what was most marked, the keen intelligence, musical feeling, high standard as to program, or perfection of performance. He always played the accompaniments (even when singing himself), while her lovely voice was one never to forget. They gave concerts from St. Petersburg to Rome, from Boston to San Francisco, and taught people everywhere what could be the result of natural gifts plus the passion for perfection that ought to be the characteristic of the real artist. As they were uncompromising in their standard, I have always felt that her singing of my " Irish Folk Song " was one of the truest compliments I ever had. My friend of many years, Max Heinrich, was another who played the piano accompaniments to his own singing, while to him is due the popularity of my " Land o' the Leal."

To return to London: This year we also saw something of the Ian Robertsons, with whom we were to become still more intimate in later years. One of the things dearly remembered from that summer is the four young girls (then about fourteen), Beatrice Forbes-Robertson, Louise Drew,[1] Helen Henschel, and our daughter; while the stories of their different

1 Daughter of the distinguished actor, John Drew.

[72]

lives since then would be interesting to relate. We wished to go, after London, to some seaside place that was not a resort, and, by a lucky chance, the little town of Hythe was suggested by Bispham. Hythe, four miles from Folkestone, is one of the Cinque Ports, off the beaten track. Thackeray, in his last and unfinished work " Denis Duval," gives a vivid and faithful picture of these towns in the latter part of the Eighteenth Century.

We had a maid who had served in hotels. To show how little we Americans know about proper tipping, we asked her what ought to be given weekly to the headwaiter in the hotel, and were told, as I remember, three shillings for our party of five people. We could hardly believe her; and I was as much relieved as astonished to find, after giving him this small amount at the end of the first week, that he was perfectly satisfied, respecting us, in fact, as knowing our business. At the hotel we came across a characteristic English attitude towards people " in trade." The manager was a Major Logan, who had married the daughter of one of the shopkeepers of the place, and, although not superior to her in any way, was considered to have lowered himself permanently by so doing.

Hythe was especially interesting because of the school of musketry there, the Martello towers (built in the Napoleonic days), and the military canal several miles long, constructed at the same time. There were several Roman castles in the neighborhood, some in ruins, and others restored and lived in. We visited one of these (now a farm-house), and from some ruins on the place I took away a tile, which had been there for at least a thousand years. At Hythe I saw my first golf-links. It is hard to believe that at this time the game was little known to us at home. Today how many millions are spent on it! I had a room in a house in the town away from the hotel, hiring a piano, and doing piano work as well as finishing an orchestral suite, which Paur played the next year. To show how oddly people encounter one another over there, one day we were walking in the neighborhood of Sandgate, the town lying between Hythe and Folkestone, when, on turning a corner, lo and behold! the Henry M. Rogers', who had been staying at a town a dozen miles away from us. To the men who were at the hotel (almost all business men), I was evidently a godsend as an American who must be able to answer their questions as to Atchison, Erie, New York Central, etc. It was then that I first realized how the doubtful things, such as Erie, were absorbed by English investors blindly. We left Hythe with reluctance, since my holiday was nearing its end, and took the boat at Folkestone for Boulogne and Paris, in this journey having a first experience of what it was to travel on the continent with a lot of luggage. For there was nearly twenty dollars to pay for excess weight. We had to get used to this.

Hythe had been a perfect summer climate, so that it was doubly hard to plunge into one of the hottest ten days I have ever known. The journey to Paris was purgatory, and from our arrival until my departure much of the time was spent in our rooms at the Continental. How well I remember those broiling mornings, when I would go out to take my coffee at some neighboring restaurant, buying a peach on the way for fifteen cents. We went one day to the Eiffel Tower for lunch. All the theatres were impossible on account of the heat, and at that time I was hardly aware of the pleasure afforded by the Bateaux-mouches. If we had known, we could have had pleasant hours in this way.

IX · TRAVELS (continued)

AFTER ABOUT TEN DAYS OF THE CITY, I WAS OBLIGED
to return to Boston (thus early because of the church
opening), and, with my sister's daughter, Amelia
Tileston, went to Brussels and Antwerp, where we
took the Red Star steamer. New York was equally
hot. After a summer without mosquitoes, I hardly
knew what the mosquito-netting above my bed in the
hotel was, to be reminded later in the usual way. The
family stayed over for the winter, going to Meran,
now, alas! not in the *Austrian* Tyrol, and with its
name changed to Merano. In Boston I went into lodgings at 96 Mount Vernon Street, and there I stayed
until 1897, finding the St. Botolph Club very convenient for meals. As to the next winter, there is nothing to be said except that, no longer having a house,
I was obliged to have a teaching room down town,
which happened to be in the Chickering Building,
where Lang and others were.

And so the winter passed, the end of May came,
and I was off, this time to rejoin my dear ones, who
had been having eight months in one of the most attractive places to be found. On the way to them I took
perhaps two weeks for London and a week for Paris.

In London I found the Kneisel Quartet already in lodgings on the same street as Henschel; and so I took a room in the neighborhood to be near all these friends. The Kneisels were giving concerts in London with real success (among other things, a new MS. quartet by Henschel) , and I feel sure would have been able to make this visit an annual one; but they were prevented from returning again until 1904, when the tragedy of Kneisel's boy, Robert, brought them hurriedly home in the midst of the tour they had untertaken that summer, and effectively ended the idea of their going so far from their families. One very pleasant occasion was when Henschel had the Quartet and me to luncheon at the Garrick Club; for me particularly, as its name was so familiar. As great admirers of Hans Richter the Quartet was delighted to be able to go to his concerts (in the old St. James Hall) . As for Kneisel (and me) , Richter, and Thomas were the ideal conductors. Simple in methods, big musically, with the highest ideals, and at their best in the finest music, I think Thomas perhaps more varied in his ability. Richter (naturally) , I had first known as a conductor at Bayreuth in 1878, when the orchestra was composed of the pick of German players, who regarded it as an honor to take part.

One curious experience there, by the way: Lang and I were looking about behind the scenes (it was between acts of " Götterdämmerung "; how we happened to be allowed there I cannot remember). When the trumpets and trombones outside gave the signal that the next act was about to begin, we had the boldness to stay on, and, in a few minutes, when the orchestra had assembled, to sneak in by the little door by which they had entered. So there we were, in the orchestra itself for the next act. The day was hot, everyone being in shirt-sleeves, and we could see how differently the majestic Richter behaved (the orchestra being quite out of sight of the audience). He shouted to different players and to the singers, gave them cues, and was quite a different person from the one we were used to seeing in the concert room. It was a remarkable experience. We were observed sitting in our corner, but the liberty we had taken was winked at.

At one of the London concerts to which the Kneisels went, the Tschaikowsky " Pathetic " was played. Now this had been given by the Boston Orchestra several times in the year or so previous to 1896 with enormous success and splendidly by Paur, who, though not a conductor of much refinement (I should hate to hear him try Debussy), did do remarkable things with works of a grandiose sort and of an emotional nature. He was, however, not much respected by his orchestra and underestimated by it. At

this Richter concert the four of the Kneisel Quartet
and I were in a row very near the stage, and all in a
reverential way looking forward to the great Richter
and what he would do with the Tschaikowsky. But
as one movement succeeded another a blank look of
dismay appeared on the faces of the quartet, for the
work was one with which Richter evidently had little
sympathy, and at the end Kneisel and the others had
to remark, " Well, old man Paur is better than we
thought he was." It's odd what poor results a first-rate
conductor sometimes gets with a work for which he
does not care. This Symphony, for example, with
Gericke and Monteux, two splendid and above all
conscientious conductors, I remember as incredibly
dull, while Muck's performance of the Schumann
Symphony in B-flat stands out in my memory as one
of the poorest things conceivable.

I enjoyed my days with Henschel and the Kneisels,
but was glad, after a week in Paris, to find myself on
the train for Basle, Innsbruck, and finally Meran.
This was one of the most beautiful journeys possible,
especially in the part from Basle to picturesque Innsbruck, and over the Brenner Pass to Bozen, where I
was met by my wife's mother, with whom I made the
last lap of my journey, ten miles by railway, in a sort
of country new to me. How odd it was to walk with
her through the Meran streets, and to find myself

[79]

finally opposite the Villa Platter, and, best of all, to see the dear faces of my wife and daughter.

Their apartment was in the highest part of Meran called Obermais. The recollection of the summer was to be one of the precious possessions of my later years, for the never-trodden ways made the impressions stronger and more lasting. Arrangements had been made to go to a hotel on the Mendel-pass, so, after a few days of mountain walks and entrancing views of valleys and castles, we left Meran to go up the mountain, which at that time was not scaled by a railway. We took an early train, breakfasted at a little village (Sigmundskron) , and, after a drive to another farther up the mountain (Eppan) , we began our climb of three hours by the mountain paths. At Eppan I remember a queer sort of notice painted on the side of the little hotel: " Beer, Wine, Billiard, Stabling, Piano," etc. The ascent is naturally shorter up over the mountain than by the fine, contour, military road, that takes five hours to the top by diligence and three to come down. In doing this latter for a good deal of the time the horses do not pull at all, gravity causing the carriage to descend, while a sort of shoe is attached to the rear by a rope, to act as a brake by scraping along on the surface of the road.

We had very pleasant rooms in the *dépendance* of the hotel, and I wrote like a good one, for a piano had been sent up from Bozen (Bolzano) . What especially pleased me was some pieces for the left hand (one of which, a Prelude, is practical and effective; the other two, as I find now, horribly awkward to play) . There were several women from Vienna and Graz who were good musicians and very knowing about the literature of music; but in that way we in Boston were much ahead of them, for when I showed them the score of the Tschaikowsky " Pathetic " Symphony, with the remark that we had already heard it in Boston several times in successive years, they could hardly believe me, since they had not yet had that opportunity. It was the same with some of Brahms' pieces from his Op. 117 and 118.

We were in the Welsch Tyrol, " the foreign Tyrol," the mountainous part of Lombardy, given by Italy to Austria by the Treaty of Trent, and could realize how many of the people idealized and worshipped Italy and hoped for repatriation. Austria treated her acquisition with tact and generosity, in contrast with the policy of Italy in the German Tyrol, when that came to her after the Great War. In the Welsch Tyrol at that time each village was allowed to choose its language, and the Austrian Government provided instruction in the language chosen, German or Italian. As to this, it is curious to reflect on Mr. Wilson's remark, when this matter came up at

Versailles, " Do the Tyrolese speak German at all? " Of course, the language of the true Tyrol is German, but the Welsch Tyrol, the " foreign Tyrol," had been Lombardy, Italy; and naturally only a few villages were German, people living near the border who had drifted together.

The summer came to its end too soon, for in early September I was forced to go home, leaving my wife and daughter. I have never left a place, probably forever, with such reluctance; and when, on the journey to Munich, the mountains of the Tyrol gradually faded away from the horizon, a great longing came over me. If one loves the mountains it is always dispiriting to come down to the plain. After the events of ten years ago, the most interesting thing about the rest of the journey to London is that we passed through Strasbourg, Luxembourg, Ostend, etc., a part of the world with which we were later to associate so much that is terrible.

The next winter (1896) was uneventful, its chief feature for me being the performance of my Suite in D minor (practically a symphony) from MS. by Paur. In it there was a considerable gain in handling the orchestra. Its fortune has been the usual one of American compositions of its sort. It had a few first performances by orchestras here (and one in England by Henry J. Wood), and afterwards little chance. The movement in variation form really satisfied me.

For the next summer I again went to Europe to rejoin my wife and daughter. In Paris, how well I remember waiting in the Gare du Nord that afternoon when my two were coming on the Cologne express, and what it meant to see theirs in the crowd of faces. We were together a few days in Paris at the moment of the "retour de Longchamps," and the spectacle given by the drive of President Faure from the Gare du Nord to the Place de la Concorde, on his return from Russia. One can hardly realize today the joy that this apparently impregnable alliance with Russia gave to France, nor how this confidence led people to put their savings, as a perfect security, into Russian investments.

We wished to spend the summer not in Paris but in one of the delightful suburbs; and, following a suggestion of our friend, Helen Hopekirk, went one day to a sort of restaurant-hotel in Meudon for luncheon, and to find out whether it would turn out to be the sort of thing we desired. But it was too remote, in the woods, a long way from the railway and river-boats; so this idea had to be given up. But by good luck, as we stopped at one of the riverside hotels at Bas-Meudon, my wife, noticing that it had an annex, asked to look at rooms. The upper story was five rooms in a row, just what we needed, and the price fifty francs, not a day but a *week*. Meals were at a similar rate. The result was ten delightful and unusual weeks (incidentally the cheapest I have ever known, although comfortable in every way). We had a fine view of the Seine from our windows, and, almost at the door, the landing of the steamboat. One could also go by railway or by trolley; so that there was a variety of pleasant ways to get to Paris, and when one wished a change it was easy to go in for the day.

We also saw in this little town something of the ordinary French life in such a place, so remote in spirit from the American Colony in Paris. The housekeeper had been a model for Gérome in her youth, and told us about groups of artists from Paris who came to this restaurant fortnightly in the summer, speaking in familiar terms of some of them. We realized the charm of this one evening when, sitting with Paul Viardot, the violinist, who had come out to dine with us, he exclaimed, "Tenez, voilà Dubois et Lenepveu!" and went forward to meet a number of men who were entering the place, musicians who came there for such dinners through the summer.

Some years previously Paul Viardot and some others had played my Piano Quartet in Paris (an unusual compliment naturally), and I had hunted him up as soon as we were settled for the summer.

[84]

Through him I was asked to come, when I wished, to some musical evenings which occurred every week in the rue Ballu in the St. Lazare quarter at the house of a rich amateur, who had a beautiful music room, where a number of amateur and professional musicians came to make music. I went twice to these meetings, playing the piano part in my Quartet and the Violin Sonata, not only having an exceedingly pleasant time, but getting a real little peep into the musical life of Paris that is so rich and varied.

I worked really a great deal, playing, practising, and writing; for this was a fruitful summer as to composition, and a lot of songs and piano things came to their birth. I often went into the town for the opera, etc.; while one evening Kitty and Katharine went to a performance of " Un Sogno di Mattina di Primavera " and " La Locandiera " by Duse (I forget what I was doing that evening) ; but we all drove out at a very late hour by the road on the left bank, a rather eerie affair. In fact, when we arrived at our little town everything was singularly quiet, not a soul in sight, nor a light anywhere; but with the rôdeurs, whom we knew to be always not far away, in the woods, above, or perhaps on the bank of the river, I confess to an uncomfortable feeling.

This summer there were several people in Paris whom we knew and loved well. We saw a good deal of the Jacob Hechts and their charming nieces, Hatty and Sally Hecht and Lina Frankenstein, and their nephew, Simon Hecht. They were staying at the Hotel Chatham, and were the center of a group of talented and companionable young fellows among whose names were some often heard later; Louis Kronberg, Edgar Walter, Kaiser (I do not recall his given name), Sidney Viet, and Felix Fox. We were all together a great deal, and there was the never-to-be-forgotten celebration of our wedding anniversary at L'Ermitage in the Bois de Meudon. Mr. and Mrs. Hecht had two of the warmest hearts that ever beat, and the gift of arousing and nourishing the best and happiest emotions in those around them. On the Fourteenth, the great day, they gave a large dinner at the Chatham to a lot of us, and afterwards we mingled with the crowds in the streets and danced in the Place de l'Opéra.

Another especially good evening was when the Nevins and we dined with the Gardners at the Hotel Westminster. The Nevins were living somewhere in the Elysée quarter, and we saw what we could of them. I remember one evening when Ethelbert came out to dinner with us. He was not well, and one felt a sadness in being with him that one knows now was premonitory. Always the same lovable fellow and devoted friend, I can see him now as he stood with

Doris, his little girl, waving good-bye as our train started for Havre six weeks later. After that year he came back to the United States, to New Haven, where he died in 1901, having done so much that was beautiful in his short life. He dedicated his " Valse Gentile " to me, and I play it often amongst ourselves, and have played it in concert, as well as using it as a teaching piece. Victor Harris was also in Paris for some weeks, and used to appear on his wheel. We had known him in Boston, on his visits as accompanist for singers, and a singularly sympathetic one he was; a handsome, attractive, talented man, a charming companion and good friend, a successful teacher of singing in New York, and later a distinguished conductor of the St. Cecilia Women's Chorus there. He is the composer of some lovely songs.

Clarence Eddy, the organist, was living with his wife (a well-to-do person) at the Hotel de Calais, near the rue de la Paix, and was hospitable to us. He had quite a place among the French musicians, and we heard him one day at an organ concert at which Guilmant was present, looking on benevolently. Soon after this he and his wife separated. He must since have looked back regretfully to those days.

And so the summer went happily by, with all of us staying there, far enough away from the town to lead our own lives. It is pleasant to have a clear recollec-

AUTOBIOGRAPHY OF ARTHUR FOOTE

tion of it all today. One trip away I did take — to Bayreuth. "Meistersinger" with Richter, "Parsifal" with Mottl. Today, away from the two K's, I should hardly be happy; but at that time somehow got along perfectly well. Among others there were the Gardners and Harry and Frances Foote. One recollection (on the train coming back from Strasbourg) is that of an enthusiastic Frenchman in my compartment with a copy of the score of "Parsifal." Often I've wondered who; of the Franck lot, probably. I look back now with envy at my endurance at that time; for example, leaving Bayreuth in the morning, then via Nuremberg and Stuttgart to Carlsruhe, where I arrived at 1 A. M.; leaving the next morning at 7.30, and arriving home at Meudon at eight in the evening. Today it seems an impossible undertaking.

At about the end of our stay, Mrs. Cummin and Jack came to Paris for a while, and of course came out to us sometimes, while we made little parties to do things in Paris. We left about September 10, going to Havre for a few days, and then by "La Gascogne" to New York and home (where we were soon to be building our Dedham house). The steamer voyage, on the whole, was the pleasantest and most comfortable we had ever had; and so ended what was to prove our last European adventure together.

Looking back over the many years since our marriage, it is the summers of 1896 and 1897 that have the dearest memories; when we three were at the Mendel, and, quite as much so, when we were at Bas-Meudon. Monsieur Halloppé, our host, and his courageous struggle against diabetes; the Fraîches, housekeeper and cook — she the once sought-for model, with her painters still coming to her restaurant; the picturesque daily life of the river craft and their workers; the charming restaurant life; the carefree and colorful existence, animated by the gaiety and abounding life of Paris itself; dear friends, some gone, VALE.

X · HOME AGAIN

AFTER THE TWO YEARS ABROAD, HAVING BOUGHT some of Mrs. Albert W. Nickerson's land in Dedham, we built in 1898, and lived there until 1912. On our acre and a half we planted many spruce and other trees, which now (in 1927) have grown so much as to make the place very beautiful and picturesque. Bicycling and golf were my two pleasures. I used to go to town by train at about 8.30, getting home usually about six; in other words, I was very busy indeed with lessons.

In the eighties a number of men, among them Sam Warren and my classmates, Jack Elliot and Harry Morse, had gotten into the way of going to Dedham to play polo and hunt. Elliot later built in Needham, while Warren settled on a large, varied tract of land bordering on the Charles in Dedham, which he called "Karlstein," later a very well-known place on account of the polo field he made there. All this gave a new life to the town. At the time there was a small, unpretentious golf-club which had a nine-hole course on land now belonging to Mrs. W. G. Nickerson. All was very simple but, to a beginner (for I never even saw the game played until at Hythe in 1895), fasci-

nating. Later I joined the Dedham Country Club
and the Norfolk Golf Club (that course being at the
other end of the town), where I often played with
Arthur Thayer. The Country Club links were on
high ground, with beautiful views on all sides, good
natural hazards, and at first but nine holes. It had in
its membership practically all the people who would
naturally belong in a radius of say ten miles, and was
a center of meeting for us. My especial pal for playing there was Winslow Warren, who (it is sad to say)
usually beat me.

While in Dedham we saw it change somewhat from
the country to a suburb, although it still retains the
charm that made it exceptional among smaller towns,
as I feel strongly whenever passing through it now.
Dedham dowered us richly in friends and acquaint-
ances. The Nickersons and their wonderful hospitality in that superb " Riverdale," and at Marion we
had known before going there. Mrs. Albert Nickerson was a beautiful woman, capable and generous,
carrying on after her husband's death a difficult
burden. She had a lovely, fresh voice, well schooled,
and we both enjoyed the music we made together.
Her friendship is a precious memory, and that of her
family a present joy. The life was happy, and the summers delightful. We used always to go to Edward D.
Parsons at " The Moorland " for some weeks at Bass

[91]

Rocks, Gloucester. Its beauty and colony were a cherished part of our year.

After 1895 I had given up concert playing as a regular thing, and so there was very little of that. But I continued to compose, although most of what I did was on a smaller scale. A transcription for orchestra of the " Omar Khayyam " piano pieces (by far the most successful of my orchestral works, both in itself and in the number of performances by orchestras generally) , a Suite for string orchestra, which really satisfied me, and a Piano Trio in B-flat major, were the most important compositions of this period. The " Omar " pieces have been played twice and the Suite three times at the Boston Symphony concerts. The Trio was brought out at a Kneisel concert at Mrs. Gardner's Fenway Court in 1909, and has been reasonably successful elsewhere, although not nearly so much as my First Trio (of twenty-five years before) , which had the unusual luck of a second edition.

In the spring of 1900 I had become interested in the musical service of the Jewish Church, as described to me by Benjamin Guckenberger, a friend who had been organist at a synagogue in Birmingham, Alabama. Before beginning, it was, of course, necessary to find out the meaning of the texts and the accentuation of the words, with regard to which some rabbis of my acquaintance were so kind as to enlighten me. The picturesque service is inspiring to a composer, and I grew very keen on the undertaking. While my conscious object was to fit the music to the feeling of the words by the use of a quasi-modal system, I was unconsciously led to a wholly different sort of writing from ever before, because of the words used — an example of the fact that (as a rule) a composer will write different types of music to English, French, or Italian words. The reason is probably that accents and rhythms differ in the different languages. I always associate Gloucester with this service, for it was written there. I have heard it a few times at Jewish temples, and I have always been glad of the experience of writing it.

XI·To California

In 1911, after receiving various letters with regard to the matter from Julius R. Weber (then unknown to me, but afterwards to become valued as a friend) about work at the music school of the University of California, there came a final pressing invitation, which I accepted, to give a course of lectures in music that summer. And so, all that spring I was busy in writing twenty-four talks, whose aim was to give a comprehensive view of the history of music, with biographies of composers and with many illustrations by playing and singing. The songs, etc., were chiefly done by Miss Anna Miller Wood, my former contralto, and I played the piano in all cases. Leaving Boston towards the end of May (stopping on the way for a visit with my old pupil and dear friend, Mrs. Clay H. Hollister, at Grand Rapids), I went by way of the Union Pacific, and was met at Oakland by Julius Weber, two old pupils, and H. J. Stewart, an old friend from the days when he was organist of Trinity Church in Boston. Stewart had a car, and took me on a preliminary drive through Oakland, Piedmont, etc., leaving me in Berkeley at the little hotel, Cloyne Court, where I was to have a pleasant life for more than two months. The Pierces were my hostesses, — charming, hospitable people. From Berkeley we usually went to San Francisco by the " Key Route," part of the way by railway which terminates at the end of a mole, the rest by steamer to the Ferry Building, so familiar to those who know San Francisco.

During my stay I made many good friends, and have kept them since. Before leaving Dedham an invitation had come from H. Morse Stephens (Professor of History in the University of California) to live in his rooms at the Faculty Club, as he would be absent in the Bohemian Club all the time that I was to be at Berkeley; a rather unusual hospitality, since I did not at the time know him personally. For very obvious reasons it seemed best to decline this, however, but I never forgot his kindness. Later we saw something of him when he visited Boston, where he knew well the Barrett Wendells and Roger Merrimans. Dr. Louis Lisser, at whose house I stayed at various times, and whom I had already known through correspondence; Wallace Sabin, conductor of the Loring Club; " Bill " (W. J.) McCoy; Henry Heyman, and a lot of others — it would be impossible to exaggerate the kindness which I met at every turn. The life was a very full one for me, and it was often the last boat home to Berkeley, so that on getting back to Dedham I was pretty well tired out.

Briefly as to events outside of my work, there was a concert by the Loring Club, soon after my arrival, a part of the program being my compositions; a special service of my church music on Sunday at the Unitarian Church, at which I played the organ; a visit of a few days at Los Angeles, during which I took part in the Guild of Organists' examination of candidates for associate and fellowship. Here I was guest at concerts of the remarkable (women's singing) Lyric Club, and (men's) Orpheus Club, and saw Pasadena, Santa Monica, Hollywood, etc., through the kindness of the Walter Raymonds, who laid themselves out to make things pleasant. Later, on returning to San Francisco, I assisted the Dean of the Guild of Organists in founding a California Chapter. There was also the meeting of the California Music Teachers' Association, in which various compositions of mine were sung. One experience I could have done without, i. e. the making of speeches (in which I am very poor), for instance at the annual dinners of the Harvard Club and the Unitarian Club. I was made a temporary member of the Bohemian Club (as also of the University Club), which I enjoyed extremely, finding that it justified its reputation. How often have I wished myself again within its portals with the friends I used to meet!

At the end of my visit there happened to be the annual Grove Play, so that I had the privilege of being a guest of the Club, staying with Morse Stephens in his tent; Barrett Wendell was expected to be there with me, but his steamer from Japan arrived too late. The experience of witnessing this play, the stage being on the side of a hill, while we spectators were seated on logs in the level space below, was never to be forgotten. On the Sunday morning following, there was the usual concert marking the end of things, and in the program were movements from my Suite in D minor, which I conducted. After this came the departure, by special train, for San Francisco, and, for me, a day or two later, the road for home, by Union Pacific as far as Ogden, by Denver & Rio Grande by way of Salt Lake City and Colorado Springs, and by the Twentieth Century Limited to Boston. Dedham looked more lovely than ever in midsummer, and our house with the two in it.

The audiences for the lectures had been large (perhaps 500), and so friendly and interested that one felt instantly at home; it was there to learn and not to criticize, and so would have aided any lecturer to do his best. One felt that one was talking to a group of friends and not to strangers. I was thankful for all the hard work that had gone into the preparation of the lectures, and the pains taken to have illustrative music, for it certainly paid. When the last day came the feeling was not of a task accomplished, but of regret that it was the end of a happy experience. Besides these lectures, by the way, there was a course in Harmony, the attendance upon which was naturally much smaller. Since that year various people have gone to the University of California summer school in the same manner — Horatio Parker and Chadwick; while in 1914 I had agreed to return and practically to repeat 1911, but was prevented by an operation for appendicitis. David Stanley Smith went in my place.

Just before leaving, I was asked to come as the head of the music department of the University, for so far it had not amounted to much. Recognizing this, President Wheeler wished to get some musician of standing and of more than local reputation to organize and put it on a sound musical basis. I had so fallen in love with California and the life there, everything I felt about me was so sympathetic and hopeful, and the opportunity for constructive work was so great and inviting that it was hard to decline. But the work ahead in that case would have been tremendous, demanding a younger man than I, and the roots had

[98]

gone too deep during the more than fifty years to make transplanting best, while the day was soon coming when work ought to be lessened and not increased, if one were able to bring that about. I have therefore never regretted the decision to remain in Boston, although I had really a strong desire to go to Berkeley for the remaining years of a professional life.

XII·Town and Country

One day during my visit to california i re-ceived a telegram telling me of a house in Brookline which my family thought would be just the thing for us; for we had been coming to the conclusion that it would be better to leave Dedham, much as we loved it, and to live nearer Boston (there were several rea-sons for this) . I answered the telegram with " yes "; so that the house at 81 Green Street, Coolidge Cor-ner, was bought, and to it we removed in 1912. While we were so near Boston that a half hour's walk brought one to Massachusetts Avenue, the neighbor-hood when we went there was charming and quiet. All this, however, was soon changed by the building of numberless apartment houses and the annoyance of increasing traffic. The neighborhood is still de-lightful, though, and our place and those of our dear friends, the Merrills and Olmsteds (for Brookline was also kind to us in the matter of friendships) , are still lovely.

I had agreed to go to Berkeley again in 1914, to re-peat the lectures of three years before, but my ap-pendicitis prevented this. As soon as I was strong enough we went down to the farm at South Hamp-

SOUTH HAMPTON, NEW HAMPSHIRE, 1928

ton, New Hampshire, which had been bought a year or so before. That summer is memorable to us on account of the great Salem fire, which we watched from where we were, twenty-five miles away, and the beginning of the World War. How little did one realize in reading the early news about the invasion of Belgium what terrible days were in store! Having lived through those years, it now seems strange that one could not have foreseen the length, barbarity, and bitterness of the struggle to come.

In the autumn of 1915 I had another illness, this time a pleuro-pneumonia which very nearly ended fatally; but wonderful medical attendance and household angels pulled me through. In 1916 Katharine went to France (afterwards to England) as a V. A. D., first at Tours and then at Chester. Among the patients at Tours was Henri Raffy, who was later to be her husband. Her letters home were the greatest source of happiness and support during our separation. They give as good a description of the hospital life there and of the feelings of the time as can be found anywhere. The joy of her getting back to us in 1918 (I think now of the necessity of her steamer's being convoyed by destroyers, and her having at hand in her stateroom a complete emergency outfit in case of wreck!) was one I need not try to describe.

After three uneventful years, December, 1920,

brought a great change. For Katharine left us, going to Constantinople to be married to Lieutenant Raffy, who was in the Armée d'Occupation there. We were then left in the Brookline house, too large for us two; so it seemed better to sell it and to try apartment life, as easier and more convenient. The apartment was a pleasant one at 102 Naples Road, only a few minutes away from Green Street, and it proved possible to give lessons there. But the less agreeable side of this way of living became apparent, and in 1925 we again moved ourselves and our possessions to 158 Ridge Avenue, Newton Centre, leaving the little corner of Brookline, where thirteen happy years had been spent. In our new house we were practically on the edge of the real country, away from bricks, with sun and air and lovely views; and one felt that as soon as one got there the city was left behind. And there we have lived ever since. In the summer of 1922 I went up from the farm (where we were as usual) to Providence to meet the Fabre Line steamer " Canada," bringing Katharine and her husband, who went back with me to Rest Harrow, where they were to live permanantly. The old, idyllic summers came again; but now we had our war hero right with us. Rest Harrow was twelve acres of varied southern upland in South Hampton and Kensington, New Hampshire, three miles from Amesbury, Massachusetts. The country was open, with wooded hills, and Hampton Beach four miles to the east. Its radiant quiet descended upon us like a blessing. Of friends and music there was no lack, and always country work to interest one.

XIII·New England Conservatory

ALTHOUGH FOR MANY YEARS (SINCE 1875) MY work had been entirely in private lessons, either at home or (after we left West Cedar Street) at a studio, it was clear, following the dangerous pneumonia in 1915, that the amount of work had better be cut down, and the studio at 6 Newbury Street given up. Lessons were therefore given at the Brookline house, and later at the Newton Centre house, when we went there from Brookline. Now, at various times I had been asked to join the faculty of the Conservatory, both in Faelten's [1] time and after Chadwick succeeded him; but had always felt that I could not accommodate myself to the ways of the place. For there one could not be one's own master in the same way as when teaching privately. But the time came when Chad's wanting me begot a wish to go to him; so that since 1923 I have had some mornings in the week at the Conservatory, enjoying the work there, and also (since 1924) giving yearly ten lectures on piano playing and teaching to the normal class. In fact, I regret today that this step was not taken many years

[1] Carl Faelten, predecessor to Chadwick as Director of the Conservatory.

ago. It is a great thing that the routine work of my profession has always been interesting, and that even now it is quite as much so, while the quality of the lessons is much better than in the past (when I thought I knew it all).

The truth is that one's standards of excellence change with the years, for better or worse; with many, especially with those who dislike the mechanical, routine side of their profession, ideals and ambitions suffer, and perceptions become blunted. One with whom this is not the case is lucky. I, as well as not a few others who came into contact with them, owe much to keen and sensitive musicians such as Otto Dresel, Henschel, Gericke, Kneisel (what a lesson it was to play with him in chamber music!) ; and the companionship of people such as Paine, Chadwick, Parker, Whiting, Converse, and Helen Hopekirk has been stimulating. Looking over their names, by the way, what would Dresel, for example, or Gericke think of the music produced today? It is not easy to keep an open mind for changes and new developments, especially when these fly in the face of all that one has cared for. But we should pray not to become so hardened in tradition as not to be honest toward what may seem to be new and perhaps not of value.

It must be confessed, however, that since 1910 a severe strain has been put upon one's willingness to be hospitable to new ideas. There has been, beyond doubt, a sweeping away of a lot of rubbish, such as the uncompromising doctrines as to consecutive fifths, cross-relations, etc.; our ideas as to key-relationships have been broadened (chiefly through Wagner) ; our feeling about form has become more elastic; knowledge of the orchestra is infinitely greater, and so on. Theory has always lagged behind practice. In fact, theory amounts to a registering of what has been accomplished (often without set purpose) by men bigger than their book knowledge. For example, in writing a book about modulation I could not find that this has had (at least in English) real discussion as regards the most important development harmonically since Bach, i.e., third-relationship of keys — an example of the stupid way in which theorists treat their subjects.

Up to (say) 1900, however, while in theory there were many senseless rules (as absurd as those depicted in the second act of " Die Meistersinger ") , it was still true that in practice these were gradually being discarded (almost unconsciously) by composers, the basic principles, however, remaining unchanged. One of those principles, e. g., that music should not be written in two or more keys simultaneously, seems to me, as a matter of simple common sense, to be so obvious as not to call for discussion. Yet polytonality (so-called) is quite the fashion today. Is it that hearing is not so sensitive as formerly? Is our feeling for logic lost? My generation cannot be too thankful for having lived when the new music came from Liszt, Wagner, Brahms, Grieg, Tschaikowsky, Dvořák, Elgar, Franck, Sibelius, Richard Strauss, Debussy, not to speak of lesser people such as Rheinberger, Rimsky-Korsakov, Rubinstein, Raff, Bargiel, Jensen, St. Saëns, Massenet, Arthur Sullivan, Johann Strauss, Sgambati. And we witnessed the sturdy beginning of a body of American composers of the calibre of Paine, MacDowell, Chadwick, Horatio Parker, Arthur Whiting, Converse, and Hadley. At the same time we were near enough to Mendelssohn, Schumann, and Chopin to regard their works pretty nearly in the class of novelties, and I even remember hearing the Schubert " Unfinished " Symphony within a year after the discovery of its MS. in Vienna. There are ups and downs in music, as in most things. That was the upswing, a wonderful period of musical creation; while we were, most of us unconsciously, living in the fifty years of most important development in music since the seventeenth century, i. e., the harmonic innovation for which Liszt (most of all), Wagner, and Brahms were chiefly responsible.

XIV·Friends and Artists

About 1915 something occurred that gave me much pleasure, for it is manna to a composer to have any of his works given public hearing by great artists, and does not happen too often. Edwin Schneider, a fine chap and gifted player, who was John McCormack's accompanist then (as now), called his attention to my " Memnon." When he sang it for the first time in Boston, and I went behind (it was at the Opera House) to introduce myself, it was the beginning of a real friendship with both of them. The world knows of John as one of the finest tenor singers of our time. But he is more than that: a musician with an extraordinary knowledge of music of all periods, always searching and browsing about, on the lookout, in libraries, etc., for what may be good, and reading through older or neglected music. Thus, at the last concert I heard, he began with an aria from Peri's " Euridice." He always had an assisting violinist or 'cellist, and constructed his programs in these groups: (1) the older music — Bach, Handel, etc.; (2) a group of modern songs; (3) one of Irish songs; (4) a final group, in which regularly one or more American songs and some merely popular ones were included.

John is genial and warm-hearted, with knowledge of the world and of people, and has really done more for American composers than any one else. Of my work he has also given a hearing (and such a hearing!) to " Through the Long Days and Years," " The Red Rose Whispers of Passion," and " The Mill " (written for him) .

Thinking of John's having liked " Memnon," brings to mind that Joseph Bonnet picked a movement from my Organ Suite out of a list of music sent to him by music publishers, as an American work which he wished to play at his concerts during his first season here. Bonnet, besides being an uncommonly fine organist, of uncompromising ideals (how he does like to play Bach, Franck, and the music of the older French, Italian, and German masters!) and the composer of some beautiful organ music as well, is a tremendous worker in preparation of programs. It was really droll to see him and Lynnwood Farnam (himself rarely assiduous in practicing) , then the organist of Emmanuel Church, where Bonnet gave some recitals. Bonnet would be working hard at the organ in the church while Farnam was practicing at the piano in the choir-room. And when they had apparently got through for the time being, it was merely to exchange occupations, Bonnet going to the choir-room and Farnam seating himself at the great organ.

And so they worked pretty well all day. Bonnet and Guilmant (who had twenty years earlier also played compositions of mine on his tours) were splendid examples of the wonderfully trained French organist, and to Guilmant especially the players who studied from 1890 on owe a very great deal, many of them having been pupils of his. One does not forget the pleasure of Bonnet's recitals, nor the imposing, majestic way in which Guilmant played his Bach.

Among those who sometimes sang songs of mine were Lillian Henschel, Gadski (who made the first record of the "Irish Folk Song"), Sembrich, Schumann-Heink, Anna Miller Wood, Mabel Garrison, Florence Macbeth, Clara Clemens Gabrilowitsch, Grace Leslie, Max Heinrich, Stephen Townsend, and Charles Bennett. To speak of all would be merely to make a list, but one that I cherish. For performances of chamber music I owe most to the Kneisel, Dannreuther, Olive Mead, and Adamowski Quartets. As to orchestral works, the early encouragement of Theodore Thomas meant everything to me; and Frederick Stock of the Chicago Symphony Orchestra, Gericke, Nikisch, Paur, Fiedler, Rabaud, Monteux, and Koussevitzky, conductors of the Boston Orchestra, and Henschel in London, have all been good to me. My friend, John Philip Sousa, has arranged two of the "Omar Khayyam" pieces for band, and given them frequent hearings. They are strikingly effective.

Let me tell something that shows the remarkable memory of Nikisch. When he first came to Boston he conducted everything without score: later, with twenty-four different programs each season, he gave this up. In 1891 he conducted from memory a MS. suite of mine, and probably never thought of it again. But when I called on him in London, four years later, he said, " You remember that suite we played? " and, sitting down at the piano, went through the first movement. I could hardly have played four measures of it. An extraordinarily gifted man he was: at sight of me the tune came right into his head. Paderewski, too, had a marvelous memory, and one afternoon, on my going behind after his concert his face lighted up, and after chiding me (I had missed a previous concert) with, " You are a bad fellow," he raised his hands slightly and played on the air, while he hummed the beginning of my Caprice in D-flat, which he had played more or less through the country.

The last thing of consequence that I wrote was two pieces for flute and strings for Georges Laurent, the superlative first flute of the Boston Orchestra. He had formed a little society called the Flute Players' Club in 1920, at whose concerts a great deal of the newer chamber music (largely with wind instruments) had been played. Monteux heard my tune at one of these concerts and asked me to rearrange it for string orchestra. This required only partial rewriting of the 'cello and occasional addition of the double bass. The piece made a real success at a Symphony concert, and Laurent of course played it exquisitely.

As to official positions, besides being for three years President of the American Guild of Organists, I was for rather more than ten years President of the Cecilia (singing) Society, for ten years President of the South End Music School, and have, since the death of Lang (in 1909) , been President of the Oliver Ditson Society for the Relief of Needy Musicians. I have also been a member of the Visiting Committee on Music at Harvard for about thirty years, and one of the judges for the Francis Boott prize in musical composition for the same period, since its founding. I am a member of the National Institute of Arts and Letters, and also, for some years, Fellow of the American Academy of Arts and Sciences. For nearly thirty years a member of the St. Botolph Club, I am now a member of the Tavern Club, of the Harvard Club, and of the Brae-Burn Country Club. In 1919 I received the degree (*honoris causa*) of Doctor of Music from Trinity College, and in 1925 the same degree from Dartmouth College.

FRIENDS AND ARTISTS

Here I must tell a wonderful thing the Guild of Organists did for me on the happy termination of my pneumonia in 1915, by causing my Festival March to be played in churches throughout the country on Thanksgiving Day of that year.

I look back with gratitude to the great number of good friends I have fortunately had among musicians, such as Gabrilowitsch, Bauer, Hutcheson, Bispham, Max Heinrich, Victor Harris, Dannreuther, Louis Lisser, W. J. McCoy, Wallace Sabin, Humphrey Stewart, Oscar Weil, Albert Elkus (these last six in California), Constantin von Sternberg, Emil Liebling, Ernest R. Kroeger, Foerster, Huss, Arthur Whiting, Converse, Rivé King, Adele Aus der Ohe, Madame Zeisler, Sturkow-Ryder, Helen Hopekirk, Katharine Goodson, von der Stucken, H. G. Tucker, Whelpley, Burdett, the Dunhams, Wallace Goodrich, the Adamowskis, Wulf Fries, Giese, Charles N. Allen, Svecenski, Maud Powell, Mrs. William Ellery (Bessie Bell Collier), Donald MacBeath, and the singers who were with me in church. To Dresel, Henschel, Chadwick, Horatio Parker, Gericke, Arthur Whiting, and Kneisel I have owed much in my musical development; for suggestions from a wise man are often of more value to one than actual instruction.

A Tribute to Arthur Foote

by

Moses Smith

*An address delivered at a memorial
concert, Lasell Junior College, Auburndale, Mass.
July 22 · 1937*

A Tribute to Arthur Foote

MANY OF YOU KNEW ARTHUR FOOTE AND KNOW HIS music far better than I, who am only beginning to learn about both. It has been my good fortune, however, recently to look into an autobiographical sketch and some of the letters which he left behind, and which have not, of course, been published. Not only what they say but the way in which they say it illuminates the character of this remarkable man. If in addition to allusions to these sources I also tell you of a few of my own little contacts with his personality, it is partly because it is so pleasant to indulge in reminiscences without the danger of being stopped, and partly because these experiences, small as they are, tell something about Arthur Foote.

It must be almost twenty years ago, when Arthur Foote was little more than a name for me, that I happened to run across his little booklet, "Some Practical Things in Piano Playing." Some things in it made so marked an impression on me that, although I have scarcely seen it since, I have never forgotten them. Of especial importance to me at the time was what Foote had to say about sight-reading at the piano and the importance, as well as method, of freeing oneself from the slavishness of constant visual reference to the keyboard. These two aspects of pianism, which are, of course, closely related, were my principal weaknesses, as they still are for so many poor or even otherwise good pianists. Stimulated by Foote's remarks I was enabled, within a single summer, if not entirely to cure myself of the weaknesses, at least to make rapid progress toward conquering them. It was not, very likely, that Foote had anything new or revolutionary to write on these subjects, but rather that his exposition of them was so clear, well reasoned, and forcefully simple.

Those qualities, which are so apparent in his music and in his prose style, were also the marks of his pedagogy. In the latter case they were probably due to what are ordinarily regarded as the disadvantages of his kind of education and training. Remember that Foote was not only an eminent American musician who had had no European study; he was also largely self-taught. He was, first of all, relatively old when he came to music. " When about twelve," he writes in his autobiography, " I began to show signs of interest in this (i.e., music) , being probably stimulated by my sister's lessons with Manuel Fenollosa, *the* teacher of Salem and its neighborhood. I had no especial musical inheritance or surroundings. My teacher was

Miss Fanny Paine, a pupil of Lang; the instruction-book 'Richardson's New Method' (which I now know was a really good one), and I made rapid progress. Our piano was a 'square' Chickering, with a very light but good action, my favorite show-piece being a sort of finger tremolo (rapidly repeated notes), which today I should find nearly impossible with our heavier and deeper action. But 'progress' meant merely playing notes faster; no idea of phrasing, pedalling, or expression. About two years later Miss Paine took me to Boston to play to Lang, probably with some pride; after performing the Chopin A-flat Ballade to her and my satisfaction, I remember asking Lang what those curved lines (slurs) above the notes meant: Lang sent me to Stephen A. Emery for harmony lessons at the New England Conservatory; very likely I showed him some of my attempts at composition, 'The Sands of Dee," etc. At the Conservatory there were three in my class (one of them a colored girl), while by the time we got half-way through the book (Richter), I was left alone."

The rest of Foote's formal education in music consisted of Professor John Knowles Paine's courses at Harvard — "and I owe him a great deal," Foote adds succinctly; another year of study with Paine after Foote's graduation, leading to an A.M. in music in 1875; and, quite by accident (for on leaving college Foote had had no intention of becoming a professional musician), a couple of years of organ and piano study with B. J. Lang — the " Lang " already referred to. That was the sum of his formal training, if a few lessons with Stephen Heller on the Continent and perhaps some other instruction more in the nature of advice be excluded. And it should be remembered that the mere fact of solicitation of advice or accepting it when offered is a form of self-instruction.

Such a relatively unorganized musical education would be a great handicap to a mediocre person devoting himself to teaching, as Foote began to do as early as 1876. For a first-rate intellect, however, such a background had its positive advantages. Recall the experience of Rimsky-Korsakov, who tells in his autobiography of mastering harmony and counterpoint while teaching it. A lesser figure, forced to study the day's assignment and keep one step ahead of his pupils somehow, would bluff his way through. Some of us have had experiences with such teachers, whose bluff was not too successful. But for a man like Rimsky the experience meant examining the very fundamentals of the subject with an originality and freshness that might well have been missing if he had gone through the customary academic grind. Similarly with Foote, who was able to approach the subject of piano technic, for example, with open eyes, ears, and muscles; and by dint of his hard thinking and recognition of the basis of his own difficulties he was thus enabled to pose the problems in their very essence before others similarly troubled.

It is a little sad but certainly helpful for some who may be going through similar experiences to read, in Foote's autobiography, how he began to discover hitherto undreamed troubles. Discussing his studies with Lang, he says: " I was a tough case to start with; with much natural ability at the key-board, some experience, and a good deal of musical knowledge to back all of this, I only played notes, without sensitiveness or real musical feeling (like many of my pupils since) , and also played by sheer effort and will-power, being stiffer and less comfortable muscularly than any pupil I've ever had. So that it was long before I got into any kind of shape. Moreover, it was a great many years before I had real feeling for what is called ' touch.' I saw Dresel, for example, with an exquisite feeling for lovely tone and expression in playing, and admired his results without having sense to find out how he got them; and today look back with regret to the many years in which what is now to me the best side of playing was a secret to me. I was so able in some ways as to be obstinate in others, and was too well satisfied with my unsympathetic playing. On the intellectual side it was really good, but blinded me to the fact that I was wanting in the sensuous, beautiful element in piano playing, with little feeling for quality in tone and fineness in phrasing." How well the same words might be applied to some of us today, except that we never get over our obstinacy!

.   .   .   .   .   .

In more than fifteen years of professional rounds of the Boston concert-halls I used to see Foote now and then from a distance, so to say, without having much opportunity for anything more than the most casual acquaintance. The only real meeting that consisted of something more than a handshake and a " How do you do? " came one Saturday afternoon in the early Fall of 1930. The place was Commonwealth Pier, whither, as musical reporter, I had been sent to meet Georg Henschel, first conductor of the Boston Symphony Orchestra, who was returning after almost half a century to lead the Orchestra through the opening concerts of its fiftieth anniversary season. A talk with Henschel as he came off the trans-Atlantic steamer had naturally all those elements of drama and " human interest " so cherished by any reporter. But the actual " story " was even more vivid than that.

For included in the little party that greeted the

A TRIBUTE TO ARTHUR FOOTE

Henschels as they came down the plank onto noisy Commonwealth Pier were the Footes. And it seemed to be a rare, thrilling, and almost undeserved opportunity to meet and converse with two brilliant musicians, each in his own sphere, who had seen so much and lived so much, and each of whom, close to the eighty-mark, was so alert, genial, and easy to talk to. While the hand-and-motor-driven trucks beat an uneven and noisy accompaniment our talk was about another day, fifty years before, when most of us had not been born and when the people whose names had become historical landmarks were actively engaged in their daily affairs, with very likely no thought about the honor posterity would bestow on them. Henschel and Foote were of that time and stature, but here they were before me, far from " played out," still taking a keen interest in what was going on and still even taking part in those goings-on.

Foote lived on for almost seven years longer, and during that time, so far as I know, he did not cease to interest himself in the world of affairs rather than of dreams, and even to continue to exercise himself in it, although naturally in a limited way. When I assumed the position I now hold Foote began to send me notes, perhaps two or three a year, perhaps slightly more often. None was self-seeking, every one was a disinterested attempt to help me or someone else in the practice of music or in learning something about it. The notes were uniformly to the point and carefully written, usually containing a valuable item of news not readily obtainable otherwise, sometimes adorned, in addition, by the expression of a sentiment that was quite priceless.

From these little notes and from such of his writings as I have been able to examine and from my talks about Foote with people who knew him well, it has been possible to reconstruct a picture of what, for want of a word that does not come readily to hand, one may call tolerance. There was, though, in Foote's attitude nothing of the unconcern that is so often a connotation of tolerance. Foote had the rare faculty, which perhaps we must grow old to attain, of being kindly toward persons and ideas he clearly disliked. But he possessed that rare combination of intelligence, knowledge, and emotional stability which enabled him to examine the bases of his dislikes, justify them to the best of his power and then, above and beyond these things, realize the possibility of error and the advisability of postponing definitive judgment. He was not a man who vacillated from one point of view to another, like a frail leaf before the wind. Neither was he one who, arrived at a belief, hardened his mind and heart into a state of frigidity.

A Tribute to Arthur Foote

A musician of my acquaintance, for example, spent an evening with Foote a couple of years ago. By training and experience and age Foote was naturally not as sympathetic a listener to the modern harmony and polyphony of men like Stravinsky and Hindemith as those who were born fifty years later than he and who grew up with the sounds of grinding automobile brakes, the blasts of steel mills, and the hum of airplane motors in their ears. My friend, on the other hand, has been a close student of the development of contemporary music during the past twenty years. Being a Bostonian and a graduate of the New England Conservatory of Music he had sufficient common background with Foote to insure a pleasant, congenial, and informative evening.

What did they talk about? Not Foote's background of the 'eighties, but about contemporary music. It was Foote, not my friend, who led the conversation into this field. My friend was amazed by Foote's curiosity about what was happening among European composers of the advance guard, by his excellent knowledge of what was going on, and by his really sympathetic interest. They discussed Alan Berg, a composer whose training and artistic methods were at the furthest remove possible from those of Foote, and whose compositions in the twelve-tone system had been regarded as hideous monstrosities by younger men who have not had to live down a life-time of prejudice. Yet Foote's comments and questions were in the same vein of kindly interest and tolerance and alert curiosity.

.   .   .   .   .   .

Thus Foote, in a life that exceeded eight decades and was well in the ninth, did not grow old in the usual sense. The " natural " way, as we say glibly, is for a man's mental arteries to begin to harden, often as early as fifty; for his spirit to congeal, so that the only values remaining to him are the values of his youth. The really natural way, though, is the exceptional way of a man like Foote, who at eighty could understand and sympathize with other people's ideals even though they were remote from his own. He had lived his life and was still living it; but he did not presume to judge the pattern that the lives of others who came after him should take.

As to his own life and more particularly his music we must recall the obvious; like most sentient beings, including even genius, he was a man of his time. When we say that, we are prone to forget that what the expression means is a man of the time of his youth. What men live by is what they have learned in youth. In rare cases, like Foote's, they are capable of following their own line of development while leaving plenty of room on the road, so to say, for others. In

[126]

most cases, as I have just indicated, they want to be, in their old age, road-hogs.

What was Foote's time? He was born on March 5, 1853, in Salem, Massachusetts, where he grew to young manhood and whence he went to Harvard College in the early 'seventies. And so Foote's time was the 'seventies and 'eighties, when he was shaping his life into the form it was more or less to have until he died on April 8 of this year.[1] He was thus a member of that group of first important, representative composers of this country, a group that centered more or less in Boston and that included Chadwick, MacDowell, Horatio Parker, and others. He outlived most of that group by many years; and that is why we are likely to forget the number of his page in our musical history. It will again be helpful, in charting our chronology, if we remember that the first important literary group of representative Americans, also centering in Boston, included Lowell, Longfellow, Hawthorne, Emerson, and so forth. This group, it is true, came a little earlier than the musical one; a circumstance that may be more than a coincidence, if we examine, on the Continent, how various artistic movements reached literary expression usually a little before musical.

If we divide our leading American composers into

[1] (1937)

generations — a procedure that can be helpful if not always accurate — then we may call John Knowles Paine of Harvard the great-grandfather, sire of the line. Such an appellation is a little more than merely metaphorical because of Paine's influence on the following group, especially, as we know, on Foote. Following this genealogical analogy further, we could include as the fathers of our present generation men like John Alden Carpenter, Edward Burlingame Hill, Rubin Goldmark, and so on. The present generation contains more radically-minded men like Roy Harris, Aaron Copland, Walter Piston, and others. Times move so rapidly, though, that even these men are rapidly becoming fathers, not so much by dint of any positive action of their own as by the simple fact of others growing up.

And so, instead of regarding Foote as a composer of our time merely because by longevity he lived into it, we will arrive at a better understanding of his music and his position in American musical history if we note such a document as a letter of Ethelbert Nevin, written to his parents on January 15, 1887 (fifty years ago), from Boston, a day after he arrived here. " I called," he writes, " on Arthur Foote of whom I have spoken some time ago — he was as cordial as could be. I am to go around to meet his wife and babe. He is the most promising of the rising musicians, and I'm getting in with the lot." We New Englanders, you see, among whom Foote still seems to walk, have to rub our eyes on realization of the fact that Foote was older than the long-departed Nevin and that half a century ago he was " the most promising of the rising musicians."

We must therefore listen to Foote's music with the ears that we apply to Chadwick's and MacDowell's. To attune to it an ear employed for American music of our time would be sheer nonsense. This is not to belittle Foote's music. It rather raises it in our estimation that we are able to say he was a composer of his time and scene. Beethoven's music was of his time and place; Bach's was, too, if we take into account certain circumstances. The composer who is not likely to live is he who writes only in the past, and does not hear the sounds of his own time. If he writes truly in the present, he need not worry about the future; that will take care of itself.

We may say of Foote what another, himself a world-famous composer, said on the recent occasion of the death of George Gershwin. No one, it would seem on superficial examination, could be further in ideals and practice from Gershwin than Arnold Schoenberg, the Austrian composer, founder of the twelve-tone school, now living in Hollywood. At a ceremonial broadcast on the radio from there a day or two after

Gershwin died Schoenberg spoke just a few sentences. But they were enough in which he could salute the departed scion of Tin Pan Alley " as a great composer, because he sang the songs of his people and of his day." . . . I can think of no more fitting tribute to the memory of Arthur Foote.

Homage to Arthur Foote

by
Frederick Jacobi
in *Modern Music*, May–June 1937

2

HOMAGE TO ARTHUR FOOTE

In ARTHUR FOOTE, AMERICAN MUSIC HAS LOST ITS LAST Victorian. Though born in 1853, Foote was scarcely influenced by any music later than that of Mendelssohn. Of romanticism we find comparatively few traces; of impressionism and that which has followed, none.

In life, Foote survived our great romantic, Mac-Dowell, and our impressionist, Loeffler. How it would have astonished the latter to think that in this day of ours both his music and that of Foote, who must have seemed to him an almost hopeless traditionalist, had slipped together into the realm of things past and that, indeed, the ratio of recession had been quite the contrary of that which might have been expected! For it is a question whether the impressionism of the one does not today seem more " dated " than the classicism of the other.

Foote cared little for " style " in the sense of " modishness." He did obviously care greatly for " style " in the sense of purity of line, clarity of structure and unity in mode of expression. He avoided everything which was out of his picture, everything which was

" trompe-l'oeil " or exaggerated. Because he was a man of culture, intelligence and taste, his music has those qualities. He was refined without being precious; he had wit and charm and his originality was expressed by the turn of a phrase, by the aggregate of his being, rather than by a striking or an arresting exterior. He was tender and his warmth showed itself through an admirable web of New England tradition: a tradition which was the base of his cult of the restrained in art. Overpowering passions were neither felt nor desired, it was an abstract, though friendly, beauty which he sought.

It will be interesting to see how long these qualities (for they are all present in his music) will continue to give pleasure to the public. It has, in any event, been significant and elucidating to note the success which greeted Dr. Koussevitzky's revival with the Boston Symphony Orchestra this year of his *Suite in E-major* for strings. Here was no mere " tribute to a senescent colleague," no mere archaeological excavation. The public, at its many repetitions (both in the concert hall and over the radio) , did not fail to show that they were delighted with the work. It was not Americanism in Music, not Modernism in Music, nor even Archaism in Music. It was just music and (had they stopped to analyze) music which reflected an honest and charming individual, one who knew his craft and who had the strength and ability to express himself in an understandable and rational way.

May the memory of Arthur Foote not die from the face of American music for many years!

NOTES

PAGE NUMBER

21   Manuel Francisco Ciriaco Fenollosa, a Spanish
      musician who emigrated to the U.S. in 1838.

      Benjamin J. Lang (1837-1909), prominent Bos-
      ton teacher, pianist, and conductor. As conduc-
      tor of the Apollo Club and the Cecilia Society,
      he brought out many important works of Euro-
      pean and American composers. His daughter was
      the composer Margaret Ruthven Lang.

      No manuscripts from this early period have been
      located.

22   Ernst F. E. Richter (1808-1879), *Manual of Har-
      mony*, first translated into English in 1867.
      Foote later translated Richter's *A Treatise on
      Canon and Fugue, including the Study of Imi-
      tation* (Boston: Ditson, 1878, 1888).

24   Otto Dresel (1826-1890), German composer
      who was active in introducing German music into
      Boston concert life from 1832.

      Carl Zerrahn (1826-1909), German-American
      conductor of the Handel and Haydn Society for
      42 years and the Worcester Festivals for 31 years.
      He also conducted the Boston Philharmonic and
      Harvard Musical Association concerts, and was
      choral director for both Peace Jubilee concerts.

27   The library of the Essex Institute, Salem, Mass.,
      contains specialized collections of American
      and New England history, including material on
      Arthur Foote.

NOTES

30	The pseudonym is spelled "Fabier" on two programs dated 28 Mar 1872 and 17 Apr 1872 in Foote's scrapbook in the Harvard University Archives.
31	The Pierian Sodality, the Harvard College orchestral organization founded in 1808, was named after Pieria, legendary birthplace of the Muses. Former Pierians founded the Harvard Musical Association in 1837 (see note for p.40).
32	*Class Song,* printed in the *Harvard Advocate* 17 (18 June 1874), 153.
33	These early manuscripts have not been identified or located.
35	Franz Kneisel (1865-1926), Rumanian-born concertmaster of the Boston Symphony Orchestra and founder of the Kneisel Quartet.
	Wilhelm Gericke (1845-1925), who twice came from Vienna to be conductor of the Boston Symphony Orchestra, 1884-1889 and 1898-1906.
37	The reference is probably to the *Responses for Church Use,* composed in 1895.
39	This bust was given to Trinity College, Hartford, Conn., by Foote's widow, where it has been placed in the Trinity College Archives.
40	The Harvard Musical Association is an organization composed primarily of Harvard alumni with an active interest in music (cf. note for p. 31). The Association rooms, which include a recital hall and library, are located at 57a Chestnut St. on Beacon Hill in Boston. The original entrance was around the corner at 1 West Cedar St., adjacent to Foote's longtime home at 2-3 West Cedar. The library's holdings contain Foote holographs bound together with his personal copies of published works, as well as a photograph of Foote presented by his widow. Other

NOTES

memorabilia in the room bear evidence of Foote's active interest in the HMA.

William F. Apthorp (1848-1913), music critic of the Boston Evening Transcript and annotator of the Boston Symphony Orchestra programs.

44   The world premiere of the Tschaikovsky Concerto was in Boston on 25 Oct 1875.

46   Kneisel died in 1926, not 1925.

Helen Kopekirk Wilson (1865-1945), Scottish pianist who lived in Boston from 1897 and taught at the New England Conservatory.

47   Templeton Strong (1856-1948), American composer who lived most of his life in Europe.

49   On p. 104 Foote states he began teaching at the New England Conservatory in 1923.

51   No true second edition of the *Trio*, op. 5 has been located, although Foote's personal copy in the Harvard Musical Association is inscribed with the date 1926. He makes another reference to a second edition on p. 92.

The *Second Trio*, op. 65 is in B-flat major.

The *Quartet*, op. 23 and the *Quintet*, op. 38 are for piano and strings.

52   Foote often referred to Annette Essipoff's "American" program on 12 May 1877 as the beginning of American music performances.

55   Whiting went to New York in 1895, Parker to New Haven in 1894.

55-56   Foote's first published works were the *Drei Stücke für Pianoforte und Violoncell*, op. 1 and *Trois morceaux de piano*, op. 3.

56   The *Serenade in E dur für Streichorchester*, op. 25 is a reworking of the *Suite for string orches-*

[139]

tra in E, op. 12 and movements of the *Suite No. 2 for string orchestra* in D, op. 31.

57   Foote wrote both the Quartet, op. 23 and the *Symphonischer prolog: "Francesca da Rimini,"* op. 24 in 1890 while vacationing at Mrs. Gardner's summer home in Beverly, Mass.

67   Foote's first significant composition was the *Trio für Pianoforte, Violine und Violoncell in C moll,* op. 5.

72   "Land o' the Leal" was published as *I'm wearing awa',* op. 13, no. 2.

74   Foote's third work for full orchestra was the *Suite in D moll für grosses orchester,* op. 36.

77   The reference to Richter in Bayreuth should read "1876."

81   The piano pieces referred to are the *Drei Stücke für die linke Hand allein,* op. 37.

82   The *Suite,* op. 36 was first performed in Boston on 6 Mar 1896.

85   Foote referred to his wife as Kitty and to his daughter as Katharine.

88   The reference is to Henry Wilder Foote, Jr. (1875-1964) and his twin sister Frances, children of Arthur Foote's brother, Henry Wilder Foote (1838-1889).

91-92   The cantata for women's voice, *Lygeia,* op. 58 and *Music for the Synagogue,* op. 53 were both written while vacationing at Gloucester (see also p. 93).

92   The Trio no. 2, op. 65 was first performed on 8 December 1908 (not 1909) at the home of Mrs. John L. Gardner on Fenway Court, now the Isabella Stewart Gardner Museum.

97	The Grove Play was the annual social and musical extravaganza put on by the Bohemian Club of San Francisco, for which the main performance was always a musico-dramatic work composed by a member of the club. See Henry F. Gilbert, "The American Composer," *The Musical Quarterly* 1/2 (Apr 1915), 176-77.
100-101	Many works were composed at the farm, called "Rest Harrow," including the little piano suite, *From Rest Harrow.*
106	The book referred to is *Modulation and Related Harmonic Questions* (Boston, NY: The Arthur P. Schmidt Co., 1919).
109	"The Mill" was published as *The Song by the Mill.*
110	There was only one disc recording of a Foote composition done during his lifetime, the one in 1908 by Johanna Gadski (1871-1932), Victor Red Seal acoustical recording no. 88117.
110-11	The catalog of the Sousa Collection at the University of Illinois lists the band arrangement of *Four Character Pieces after the Rubáiyát of Omar Khayyám,* op. 48, but the score has not been located. Cf. Foote's reference to an arrangement of one of the pieces on p. 59.
111	The Nikisch reference is to either the *Symphonischer prolog: "Francesca da Rimini,"* op. 24 on 23 Jan 1891; or the unpublished *Suite No. 2 for string orchestra in D,* op. 21 on 22 Nov 1889.
	The Paderewski reference may be to the *Caprice No. 1 in B-flat,* op. 27, no. 5.
111-12	The unpublished *Nocturne and Scherzo for flute and string quartet* had its first performance by

NOTES

Elias Hecht in San Francisco on 28 Jan 1919.
Foote later reworked this into *A Night Piece for
flute and strings,* first performed by Georges
Laurent in Boston on 13 Apr 1923.

115   Moses Smith (1901-1964), music critic for the
Boston Evening Transcript, head of Classical
Artists and Repertoire for Columbia Records,
and President of Music Press, Inc.

117   The book referred to is *Some Practical Things
in Piano Playing* (Boston, Leipzig, NY: Arthur
P. Schmidt, 1909).

125   The reference should be "Alban Berg."

131   Frederick Jacobi (1891-1952), assistant conductor of the Metropolitan Opera and professor of composition at the Juilliard School of
Music, 1936-1950.

CHRONOLOGY

1853 Arthur Foote was born on 5 March in the family home at 44 Warren Street, Salem, Massachusetts.

ca. 1865 Foote began piano study with Fanny Paine.

ca. 1867 At the suggestion of Benjamin Lang, Foote went to the New England Conservatory for harmony lessons with Stephen Emery.

1869 As a member of the Salem Oratorio Society, Foote participated in the National Peace Jubilee.

1870 After Foote graduated from Salem High School on 20 July, he entered Harvard College, where he studied counterpoint and fugue with John Knowles Paine. He lived at 49 Grays from 1871 to 1874.

1872 Foote again sang with the Salem Oratorio Society at the World Peace Jubilee. His appointment as Director of the Harvard Glee Club brought recognition to the organization for a higher level of musical attainment.

1874 On 30 March Foote was elected to Phi Beta Kappa and in June received a B.A. from Harvard College. During the summer he began piano and organ study with Benjamin Lang.

1875 Harvard granted Foote the first M.A. in music to be given by an American university. In August he began his professional career, opening a studio for the teaching of piano. On 17 January he joined the Harvard Musical Association, a membership he retained throughout his life.

1876 Foote made his piano recital debut in Boston and was appointed organist at the Church of the Disciples. In May he went to the Centennial Exposition in Philadelphia, after which he traveled to Europe to attend the first

Bayreuth Festival and premiere of the complete *Ring des Nibelungen.*

1877   On 12 May Annette Essipoff presented a program of American piano music in Boston and included Foote's *Gavotte,* op. 3, no. 2, signaling the first public performance of one of his compositions.

1878   Foote made his second trip to Europe during the summer and attended the Paris Exposition. In October he was appointed organist and choirmaster of First Church Unitarian, a post he held until April 1910.

1879   Foote was appointed to the program committee of the Harvard Musical Association. During the summer he again traveled in Europe, continuing to make and renew acquaintanceships with many prominent musicians.

1880   On 10 March Foote presented the first in a series of chamber music concerts in Boston which continued until *ca.* 1895. On 7 July he married Kate Grant Knowlton, and shortly thereafter took up residence at 2-3 West Cedar Street on Beacon Hill in Boston, where he lived and taught until 1895.

1881   The Footes' only child, Katharine, was born on 26 September.

1882   The first of Foote's compositions to be published, *Drei Stücke für Pianoforte und Violoncell,* op. 1 and *Trois morceaux de piano,* op. 3 were issued jointly by August Cranz (Hamburg) and Arthur P. Schmidt (Boston).

1883   Foote and his family spent the summer in Neuilly, France, where he completed the *Cinq pièces de piano,* op. 6, dedicated to Stephen Heller, with whom Foote studied briefly. On 10 November Foote appeared as piano soloist with the Boston Symphony Orchestra, the first of eight such appearances.

1884   In July Foote attended his national convention of the Music Teachers' National Association, an organization which honored him with a life membership in 1905.

CHRONOLOGY

1886   The first of many performances by the Boston Symphony Orchestra occurred on 15 May, when Wilhelm Gericke conducted the premiere of Foote's *Suite for string orchestra in E major,* op. 12.

1888   Foote and his family spent the summer in Paris, during which time he again attended the Bayreuth Festival.

1889   While Foote summered on Nantucket Island, he wrote the *Suite No. 2 for string orchestra in D,* op. 21, which received its first performance on 22 November by the Boston Symphony Orchestra with Arthur Nikisch conducting.

1890   During a summer vacation spent at Isabella Stewart Gardner's home in Pride's Crossing, Beverly, Massachussets, Foote completed the *Symphonischer prolog: "Francesca da Rimini,"* op. 24 and the *Quartet in C dur für Klavier, Violine, Bratsche und Violoncell,* op. 23.

1891   Foote spent the summer in Hull, Massachusetts, where he composed *The Skeleton in Armor,* op. 28. He also wrote his two most popular works, the *Songs,* op. 26 and *An Irish Folk Song,* both of which appeared in numerous editions in this country and abroad.

1893   Foote attended the Columbian Exposition in Chicago, where he performed the *Piano Quartet,* op. 23 with the Kneisel Quartet, and conducted the Theodore Thomas Orchestra in a performance of the *Serenade in E dur für Streichorchester,* op. 25. He again vacationed in Beverly, Massachusetts, where he completed the *Quartet for strings in E minor,* op. 32 and the *Concerto for Violoncello and Orchestra,* op. 33.

1895   The Footes spent the summer in London and Hythe, England, where he completed the *Suite in D moll für grosses orchester,* op. 36. His wife and daughter remained abroad for two years, during which time Foote lived at 96b Mt. Vernon Street, took his meals at the St. Botolph Club, and maintained a teaching studio in the Chickering Building.

1896   Foote joined his family in Europe, spending the summer in the Mendel Pass near Bolzano.

1897   On his last trip to Europe, Foote spent a productive summer in Bas Meudon, France, returning to Bayreuth for two performances.

1898   Foote was honored by election to the National Institute of Arts and Letters. The success of his many publications enabled him to build a home in Dedham, Massachusetts, where he lived until 1912.

1900   Foote composed the *Music for the Synagogue,* op. 53 during the summer at Gloucester, Massachusetts.

1905   Arthur P. Schmidt published *Modern Harmony in its Theory and Practice,* which Foote jointly authored with Walter R. Spalding. It went into three editions and numerous printings during Foote's lifetime, and was reissued in 1969 by Summy-Birchard Co., holder of the rights to the Schmidt catalog.

1907   On 13 December the *Four Character Pieces after the Rubáiyát of Omar Khayyám,* op. 48 received its first performance by the Chicago Orchestra, Frederick Stock conducting. This work, which Foote considered his most successful for orchestra, was arranged from the piano pieces, *Five Poems after Omar Khayyám,* op. 41.

1909   Foote was elected national president of the American Guild of Organists, serving until 1912. The premiere of his best-known orchestral work, the *Suite in E dur für Streichorchester,* op. 63 took place on 16 April with Max Fiedler conducting the Boston Symphony Orchestra.

1911   Foote spent the summer as acting chairman of the music department and guest lecturer at the University of California at Berkeley, declining an offer to remain there permanently.

1912   Foote sold his home in Dedham, moved to 81 Green Street at Coolidge Corner in Brookline, Massachusetts, and purchased a farm in South Hampton, New Hampshire, which he called "Rest Harrow." He also moved his studio to 6 Newbury Street, where he taught until 1915, after which time he taught at home.

1913   On 14 May Foote was made a Fellow of the American Academy of Arts and Sciences.

1914   On 2 December Foote was elected an honorary member of Phi Mu Alpha-Sinfonia.

1915   A nationwide expression of gratitude for Foote's recovery from pneumonia occurred on Thanksgiving Day, when members of the American Guild of Organists performed his "Festival March," op. 29, no. 1 during Thanksgiving Day services.

1919   Foote received an honorary D.M. from Trinity College, Hartford, Connecticut, and Schmidt published *Modulation and Related Harmonic Questions.* On 28 January his *Nocturne and Scherzo for flute and string quartet* (later reworked into *A Night Piece)* was performed in San Francisco.

1920   Katharine Foote was married in Istanbul to Henri Raffy of Agen, France. They returned to live at Rest Harrow from 1922 until 1927, when they moved to Kezar Falls, Maine.

1921   Foote moved to 102 Naples Road in Brookline, and began teaching at the New England Conservatory, a post he held until his death. To commemorate his association with the Conservatory, his daughter established the Foote Scholarship for an outstanding student of piano or organ. In 1950 a bust of Foote was presented to the Conservatory by the sculptress, Bashka Paeff, and placed at the entrance of Jordan Hall.

1923   On 13 April *A Night Piece for flute and strings* was premiered by Georges Laurent and the Boston Symphony Orchestra, Pierre Monteux conducting.

1925   Foote received an honorary D.M. from Dartmouth College and moved to 158 Ridge Avenue, Newton Centre, Massachusetts.

CHRONOLOGY

1927 Foote wrote the *Autobiography* at the request of his daughter.

1933 As an eightieth birthday gift Mrs. Edward MacDowell named a road at the MacDowell Colony, Peterborough, New Hampshire in Foote's honor. The Boston Symphony Orchestra also paid him tribute with a performance of *A Night Piece* on 9-10 March.

1937 Foote died on 8 April at Massachusetts General Hospital, Boston and was buried at Mt. Auburn Cemetery, after a successful career of more than fifty years.

1940 Foote's name was placed on the steps of the Edward Hatch Memorial Band Shell in Boston, where the Esplanade concerts of the Boston Symphony are held.

1944 Foote's wife died.

1954 Henri Raffy died.

1970 Katharine Foote Raffy died.

[148]

INDEX OF NAMES

This index, based upon the *Autobiography* only, includes those composers about whose works Foote expressed some opinion, musicians who were directly associated with him on either a personal or professional basis, and musical organizations or institutions in which Foote took an active interest. Numbers in parentheses indicate indirect references.

[149]

INDEX OF COMPOSITIONS

INDEX OF COMPOSITIONS